Diving In
to
Strategic Thinking

Gwendolyn Leininger & Sandra Adams

Diving In
to
Strategic Thinking

A Teacher's Field Guide to Depth of Knowledge

Interior graphic by Christine Bursoto (p.25, 28, 137)

Cover design by Gwendolyn Leininger

Gwendolyn Leininger
Sandra Adams
Diving In to Strategic Thinking: A Teacher's Field Guide to Depth of Knowledge

ISBN-13:
978-1534688063

ISBN-10:
1534688064

First published in the United States of America by CreateSpace Independent Publishing Platform

FIRST EDITION

CONTENTS

THE AUTHORS

Gwendolyn Leininger is freelance education writer, independent editor, and public school advocate who has partnered with instructional coach Sandra Adams to compile research and co-author materials for local educators. She lives in Indiana with her husband and one daughter.

Sandra Adams is a veteran teacher, instructional coach, and entrepreneur. She was a Race to the Top team member, and she leads professional development workshops for local teachers. She lives with her husband and three daughters and is currently an instructional coach and consultant for Fort Wayne Community Schools in Indiana.

INTRODUCTION

WHY A FIELD GUIDE?

It is in the deepest waters of unexplored underwater caves that the most potential for discovery lies. But diving that deep, through dark and foggy waters, isn't easy. Diving into deep thinking is a similarly muddied task. Discussions about cognition can get very scientific and theoretical, detached from our daily experience. Depth of Knowledge (DOK) is itself a scientific categorization based on research, and although it has been presented before with many practical applications, we struggled to find a short, readable book on DOK that could be referred back to for practical use over and over again. We have written this field guide to fill that void, to bring the science of how thought processes are categorized into the realm of daily teaching practice. A field guide approach will help teachers get the most use out of the research done on DOK.

We believe that true "rigor" comes not from tougher academic standards or from changing the verbiage of instruction. What matters is what teachers do with those standards in their daily work. Teachers are the true experts, who take those academic standards and tailor them to students at all levels, guiding them through murky waters into the depths where ideas become clear. We believe a practical understanding of DOK can help teachers in that effort. We hope this book will prove a helpful tool for teachers to promote thinking and learning for all students.

A NOTE ON STYLE

We have written in plain language and avoided buzzwords or jargon because we hope DOK will prove a helpful and lasting way to view learning, not a passing educational fad. We seek to help you clarify your goals for your students and provide practical support for your professional efforts.

HOW TO USE THIS BOOK

This book is intended to be a manual and workbook whose main text can easily be read cover-to-cover but that also includes supplemental lessons, graphic organizers, and instructional frames that may be referred back to at different times in a teacher's journey. We recommend reading through it completely, but we have made every effort to break it into sections that can be understood independently from one another as well. The book is divided into 21 modules, or mini-chapters, which are grouped into 3 large sections, as follows:

Part 1: Choose To Go Deeper – This section functions as an extended introduction, using the metaphor of cave diving to explain Depth of Knowledge and challenging teachers to include more opportunities for DOK 3 and 4 in their lessons.

Part 2: Prepare for Exploration – This section introduces the elements of classroom culture that are necessary to support DOK 3 and 4 lessons.

Part 3: Dive In: Empowering Ownership – This section explains that empowering ownership of learning is the key to breaking through to levels 3 and 4. We give 5 steps you can take in your lesson design to empower ownership in your students. Each step includes detailed examples and lessons you can use and adapt.

We hope that teachers will use this book as a tool for collaboration, referring to it as they create and discuss lessons. To that end, we have included the following features:

- **In This Section** – Each of the three parts begins with a short blurb and a bulleted list of its contents, so it's easy to find what you're looking for.
- **Where Do I Stand?** – A checklist for teachers to pre-assess and discuss their individual needs before beginning each part.
- **Challenge Questions** – Each of the 21 modules features a series of Challenge Questions for teacher discussion and professional development.
- **Space for Note-Taking** – Each module provides ample space for discussion notes.
- **Takeaways** – Each part ends with a list of important points to remember. We hope the takeaways will simplify Depth of Knowledge and allow teachers to put their understanding into practice.

1
CHOOSE TO GO DEEPER

This section of the book provides a basic understanding of Depth of Knowledge, explains how DOK is misunderstood, and shows the need for educators to expand their teaching to include all levels. It also identifies a "toxic" zone where many teachers get stuck, unable to break through to levels 3 and 4.

In This Section

1. What is Depth of Knowledge?
2. The Value of DOK 1 and DOK 2
3. The Need for DOK 3 and DOK 4
4. Getting Unstuck: It's Not About the Verbs
5. Diving in Beyond the Word Wheel: A Metaphor
6. Breaking Through to Strategic Thinking

Where do I stand?

❏   I don't understand DOK.

❏   I am skeptical that DOK is important—it's just another educational trend.

❏   I try to teach with all DOK levels in mind, but I don't see much difference from Bloom's taxonomy.

❏   I see a need for deeper thinking in my classroom, and I want to learn how to get there.

❏   I incorporate all DOK levels in my teaching, but I don't see the benefit to students.

❏   I have successfully used all DOK levels and I have some great ideas for other teachers.

Discuss your responses with other teachers.

---

1. WHAT IS DEPTH OF KNOWLEDGE?

Sally Constructs Meaning

On Monday, a 3rd-grade student named Sally learns the definition of *evaporation* during a science lesson. Her teacher has designed the lesson so that Sally can learn the definition and see examples. Sally has "learned" evaporation, but has she constructed her own meaning of the concept?

The next morning, the sun has come out after a rain, and Sally's teacher takes the class out to the playground to examine puddles. They make close observations. They draw diagrams showing the locations of the puddles, charting how deep and wide the puddles are. They also note the air temperature, humidity, and how brightly the sun is shining. They do the same again in the afternoon, noticing how the puddles have shrunk. Sally and her classmates had already learned that as puddles evaporate they become tiny droplets of moisture in the air. But collecting the data gave them a more personalized understanding. Over the next few rainy days, Sally remembers the puddles she had measured, and she begins to notice that evaporation occurs more quickly on sunny days than on cloudy, humid ones. Friday night is spaghetti night, and Sally waits impatiently for the pot of water to boil. Her mother turns up the heat on the burner, and soon steam is rising from the pot. Sally realizes that what happens to puddles will also happen on the stove: the longer the spaghetti cooks, the less water will remain in the pot. She has taken ownership of her learning and constructed her own meaning around the concept of evaporation.

Depth of Knowledge is a paradigm for understanding the differences between Sally's Monday understanding, her Tuesday understanding, her Wednesday and Thursday understanding, and her Friday understanding. You've probably seen DOK presented in the following "word wheel." We'll discuss the pitfalls of using this wheel in module 4, but for now we just wanted to jog your memory. Look familiar?

Research scientist Norman Webb has named four Depth of Knowledge (DOK) categories, or levels of thought, for any kind of knowledge: recall, skill/concept, strategic, and extended. Here is simple explanation of each:

DOK Level	Definition	For example...
Level 1 Recall and Reproduction	Student can recall information	Learning vocabulary words
Level 2 Skills and Concepts	Student can understand information or how to perform a skill	Learning how to cross-multiply in math class; Labeling parts of speech in language arts class
Level 3 Strategic Thinking	Student can make connections they've never made before (non-routine problem solving)	Reading a multi-step word problem and determining the steps for solving it; Finding the "best answer" from several "good answers"
Level 4 Extended Strategic Thinking	Student can apply information to a new context, extending over time or across disciplines; Assimilation	Coming up with and executing an experiment, conducting independent research

Adapted from Norman Webb's DOK Overview (Webb, 2013)

When Sally learned to define the word "evaporation," that was level 1. When she collected data and saw for herself how a puddle of water becomes tiny droplets of moisture in the air, that was level 2. Level 3 happened when she realized that heat from the sun or the level of humidity in the air affects the speed of evaporation: the puddle dried up much faster on a sunny day than on a muggy, cloudy day. And level 4 was when she watched the steam rising from a pot of boiling spaghetti and understood that the hotter her mother turned up the stove burner, the more quickly the boiling water would disappear. She had assimilated the information and sifted it through her personal experience to apply it to a new context (cooking).

Sally is an imperfect example, because her story implies that the brain always moves through each DOK level in order, mastering 1 before moving to 2, and so on, like Sally did. That can be the case, but it often is not: students operate on various levels depending on the cognitive task in which they are engaged, and no one has to understand perfectly at level 2 before engaging in the thought processes of level 3. Still, seeing all four levels described in one context—Sally's understanding of evaporation—gives you an idea of how each level can look in practice.

Depth of Knowledge is a tool for examining the process of learning, and it provides a language and a frame of reference for discussing it. It is not a magic word. There's no secret trick or silver bullet lesson plan for making students learn, and that's the whole idea. You cannot construct meaning for them, but you can carve out opportunities by learning how to activate their strategic thinking skills. DOK levels 3 and 4 are about students taking ownership of the learning process. We want to help you get them there.

Challenge Questions:

1. When creating or revising lesson plans, do you consider the different levels of student thought?

2. Can you list an example of a classroom activity you use for each type of thinking?

   Level 1 Recall and Reproduction

   Level 2 Skills and Concepts

   Level 3 Short-term Strategic Thinking

   Level 4 Extended Strategic Thinking

Discuss your responses with other teachers.

2. THE VALUE OF DOK1 and DOK2

Numbering the DOK levels is somewhat misleading because in actuality they are not linear. To be clear, DOK 3 and 4 are not more important than DOK 1 and 2, nor do you have to master 1 and 2 before moving on to level 3 or 4. In fact, the deeper levels are not even necessarily more difficult. They are simply deeper because what is happening in the brain is more complex. This is an important point for teachers to remember because it means all students can work at any level, regardless of giftedness or mastery of any other level.

When we view academic standards through the lens of depth of knowledge, we see that levels 1 and 2 are expected more often in the lower grade levels, while the standards show expectations of enormous cognitive leaps between 5th and 6th grade and between 10th and 11th grade. It is imperative that we design lessons that align with the cognitive demands of the standards. Our focus in this book is helping teachers in the middle and upper grades to adopt practices that will help their students make that cognitive leap. But before we move into the DOK 3-4 focus of the rest of this book, we want to make sure everyone's on the same page with regard to DOK 1 and 2, which are essential parts of learning. It would be a mistake to try to reach DOK 3 in every lesson, or to spend all of your time extending thought to DOK 4 when some important lessons are better suited to levels 1 and 2. Before jumping into the rest of this book, look over the overviews of levels 1 and 2 on the following pages, and make sure you are striving for excellence at these levels as well.

DOK 1: Recall and Reproduction

Definition	Tasks that require students to recall or reproduce knowledge that they either know or do not know. There is no "figuring out" the answer.
Primary cognitive process	Working memory
Common questions	When did _____ happen? Who discovered _____? How would you write _____?
Common teacher behaviors	Harry Wong's procedure for teachers is a great tool for DOK 1 lessons: Model Observe Coach Acknowledge Practice, practice, practice! Reinforce (Wong, 2009)

Strive for excellence at DOK 1

Just because DOK 1 focuses on memory doesn't mean it has to be boring! Use creativity and variety to keep DOK 1 lessons fun and memorable. Which of the following tools do you use during your DOK 1 lessons?

- Collection
- Quiz
- Worksheet
- Recitation
- Show and tell
- Podcast or blog
- Timed challenges

List specific ways you could use the above tools in DOK 1 lessons.

DOK 2: Skills and Concepts

Definition	Tasks that require students to mentally process information beyond the recall level and respond to it, demonstrating that they have mentally sorted and transformed the information.
Primary cognitive processes	Organization of ideas, understanding patterns and relationships, translating information to own words
Common questions	How would you classify _____? How are _____ alike and different? How would you summarize _____?
Common teacher behaviors	Providing a graphic organizer for students to summarize or categorize information they have read, watched, or heard. **Note:** Effective note-taking during a lecture is usually DOK level 2, because students are organizing and summarizing main points. This is an important level 2 skill that will help students reach deeper levels. See module 13 for a list of note-taking systems.

Strive for excellence at DOK 2

It's easy to fall into a rut of information delivery followed by student response with common instructions like "read and summarize" or "compare and contrast." How can you use the following activities alongside those familiar favorites to help students reach DOK 2?

- Explaining or classifying photographs and illustrations
- Performing an experiment following the scientific method
- Summarizing classmates' presentations
- Watching an interview and recording important points

List specific ways you could use the above activities in DOK 2 lessons.

Keep striving for excellence as you teach at levels 1 and 2. But don't stop there. The bulk of this book will focus on levels 3 and 4 simply because we see a great need for students to learn more strategic and extended thinking skills. But we should not disregard the basic recall and understanding that is vital to education. Added to the practices above, the lesson designs in this book will help round out your students' thinking skills to engage them at all levels.

Challenge questions:

1. At what DOK level do you think you spend most of your instructional time?

2. Do you think all levels of thinking are equally important?

3. Do your students enjoy thinking at all levels, or do they seem more engaged at one level than at another?

Discuss your responses with other teachers.

3. THE NEED FOR DOK 3 and DOK 4

Most educators teach masterfully at levels 1 and 2. Now we need to complete the learning process by adding levels 3 and 4, strategic and extended strategic thinking, into our curricula. All four categories are necessary for mastery of a concept, and despite being labeled with sequential numbers they are not linear: you don't have to master one before moving on to the next. Our third grader, Sally (from module 1), could have made the same connection between the disappearance of puddles on a sunny day and the steam rising from the spaghetti pot, even if she didn't know the word "evaporation." Yet the basic Level 1 recall of the vocabulary term is an important part of the curriculum that gives her a language for solidifying her understanding, and it is no less worthy of our time than the deeper levels of thought. Instead, they are all necessary parts of a whole. This wholeness of understanding is the kind of learning that sticks. Students need practice in all four levels of thinking in order to prepare for real-world success. Opportunities to practice thinking at levels 3 and 4 are lacking in many classrooms. Here's why that matters:

Why Teach DOK 3 and 4?

Reason 1: Mastery and Real-World Application

Learning is more complete when we include opportunities for strategic and extended thinking. Students take ownership of the material when they are thinking more deeply. Making cognitive connections gives the lesson real-world meaning for the students. They are more engaged when they have thought on levels 3 and 4, so you get more interest and fewer discipline problems. We are educating students for life, so we must teach them to become lifelong learners, and that means teaching them how to make thinking their own. Strategic thinking is about moving past "I don't know the answer" to "I can figure out the answer," and life is filled with problems that don't have easy answers and require more complex thought processes. Even in the early grades we want to begin this process in order to give students every chance for success in learning.

> Strategic thinking is about moving past "I don't know the answer" to "I can figure out the answer."

If the intrinsic value of teaching students lessons they can draw from and apply throughout their lives isn't reason enough, there is also a need to prepare students for a new generation of standardized tests. Recent changes in the way many test questions are written highlight the need for expanding student thinking into levels 3 and 4. Before Common Core, 80-85% of all standardized tests were written at the "understanding" level on the well-known Bloom's taxonomy: a level that corresponds to DOK levels 1 and 2 (Hess, 2012). They tested for understanding and skills, but they didn't require students to synthesize information after deep immersion into the content. Now, since the implementation of Common Core, tests—including the newly revised SAT—expect students to think deeply at DOK level 3 and to persevere through multiple steps of text-dependent questions. Text-dependent questions are designed to "spiral" in complexity; all students in grades three through twelve are being challenged to synthesize multiple texts and justify with evidence.

Tests that once measured student thought at DOK levels 1 and 2 now require strategic thinking.

Today's tests do not rely on simple recall and understanding questions. New questions require students to justify their answers and give evidence of their thought processes, editing text to choose the best fitting word choice out of many "correct" words. The newly redesigned SAT has been billed as more "open," meaning it provides equity for all students, regardless of the disadvantages of income and minority background. This is because thinking on levels 3 and 4 removes the need for test-taking secrets and expensive test prep or tutoring; it allows students to showcase their actual thought processes.

Strategic SAT

David Coleman, president of the College Board, announced the recent redesign of the SAT with an inspiring focus on delivering a test that reflects actual classroom learning, showcases the students' best thinking work, and eliminates the need for testing tricks or jumping through hoops—no more "secrets" for passing the SAT! Instead the only "secret" is knowing how to think at the strategic level. Rather than asking tricky questions, the new SAT will measure thought processes by requiring students to...

- Justify answers with evidence
- Read and analyze a wide range of source texts, making connections across disciplines
- Analyze sequences and paragraphs for correctness and edit for effective word choice in "an extended real-world context." (This means choosing the "best" answer out of many "correct" answers.)

"What is needed is not more tests, but more opportunities," Coleman says, and the new SAT is designed to offer the opportunity for success to any student who has learned how to think, no "tricks" or expensive test prep required (https://www.youtube.com/watch?v=MSZbPJXwMI).

To allow all our students to take advantage of the more level playing field, we must help them to develop their thinking skills. Teaching in many classrooms still looks much like it did before this new focus on testing thought processes. Standardized tests have become more rigorous, but our instruction has not yet caught up in teaching these thinking skills.

The world of education suffers from an addiction to trends, and it may be tempting to write off "Depth of Knowledge" as just another new jargon and ignore the nationwide current pushing ever further toward deeper thinking skills. But unlike many educational trends, this one shows a promising focus on the cognitive development of students rather than outcomes and grades: it's truly about learning. And this "trend" shows no signs of disappearing anytime soon. If you ignore it, you risk not just your students' test scores, but their potential to become people who think. This field guide will help you round out your instruction by teaching students to think more deeply, preparing them for tests and for a life of learning.

See the Difference?

Standard

Here is one sample academic standard from the Common Core. Can you tell by reading it which DOK level it is aiming for?

CCSS.ELA-LITERACY.RL9-10.4
Determine the meaning of words and phrases as they are used in the text, including figurative and connotative meanings; analyze the cumulative impact of specific word choices on meaning and tone (e.g., how the language evokes a sense of time and place; how it sets a formal or informal tone).

Question

Now here is a corresponding text-dependent test question relating to a passage on immigration (not shown). Do you see how the test question requires strategic thinking skills?

Which of the following statements BEST describes the author's purpose for including the section "Just One Plan" in the above article?
A.   To show that Abulateef will do whatever it takes to stay in the United States
B.   To describe the long process and red tape that Iraqis must go through to stay in the United States
C.   To provide context to for understanding the plight of displaced immigrants who, despite the efforts of attorneys, are unsafe in Iraq but illegal in the United States
D.   To explain the goal of the asylum program

If you're not thinking about Depth of Knowledge when you read an academic standard, it can be hard to tell which cognitive processes are the goal. But when you look at a corresponding test question, it becomes clear that this academic standard is meant to promote strategic thinking. To be able to answer questions like these, students will need to practice strategic thinking regularly in the classroom. In module 8 we will deconstruct this same sample academic standard to show you how to identify its DOK level so you can plan a lesson around it.

Challenge Questions:

1. Have your lessons, projects, worksheets, and formative assessments changed to reflect the new focus on deeper thought, or have they stayed the same in recent years?

2. Do negative feelings about standardized testing keep you from making changes that could benefit your students?

3. Do you value some levels of thinking over others? If another teacher were to observe your classroom and count how many different DOK levels were present, would the results match your values?

Discuss your responses with other teachers.

4. GETTING UNSTUCK: IT'S NOT ABOUT THE VERBS

Take a look at that familiar word wheel again:

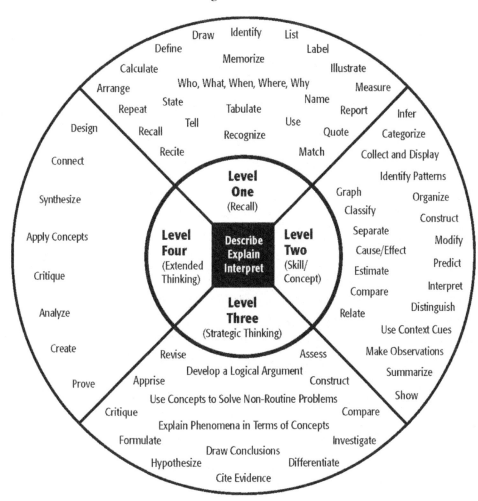

The wheel is a great illustration of how each level is a necessary part of a whole, but it also causes some problems. Many teachers, familiar with Bloom's taxonomy and its focus on verbs, get stuck looking at the verbs in the wheel. To include strategic or extended thought in their lessons, they latch onto words like "assess" or "analyze" or "create." They change their instructions to students—instead of "summarize the story," they tell students to "analyze" the story—and end up with a summary by another name.

The problem with fixating on the verbs is that the same verb can be used in any DOK level. Take a look at the examples below (Finlay, 2014).

DOK 1 - Students will <u>identify</u> essential information needed to accomplish a task.
DOK 2 - Students will <u>identify</u> information in a passage that is supported by a fact.
DOK 3 - Students will <u>identify</u> the appropriateness of an argument using supporting evidence.
DOK 4 - Students will <u>identify</u> interrelationships (themes, ideas, concepts) developed in more than one literary work.

Rather than getting caught up in the verbs, think of them instead as descriptors of what is happening in the student's brain. To move students' thought processes from one activity to another, lesson design must do more than simply telling them to "analyze" the story or "create" a timeline. It must teach their brains what it actually means to "analyze" or "create," and help them turn those activities into habits. Recognize that the verbs are the description, not the prescription. Because a student can think strategically (DOK 3) about evidence, he can *develop a logical argument*. Because a student extends her strategic thinking (DOK 4) about machines, she can *design* a better mouse trap. The italicized verbs in the above sentences are the description of the strategic DOK 3-4 thinking process, not the process itself. Keep the verbs in mind as a goal for your students, but remember that there are multiple ways of describing thought processes, so you can't rely on the verbs. You must teach them the process instead.

Verbs on a wheel can be helpful tools, just like academic standards can. But learning does not depend on verbs and standards. It depends on what teachers do with those verbs and those standards, and how they empower students to make them their own.

The DOK Spectacles

Depth of Knowledge is like a pair of eyeglasses, consisting of two interdependent parts: the frames and the lenses. The frames are more rigid, and they provide support for the lenses, making the lenses wearable and useful. The same eyeglass frames might work for almost anyone, but the prescription of the lenses must fit the individual who is looking through them. In the same way, teachers can use DOK as a frame: a way to understand cognitive processes and to structure lesson plans for a whole class of students. But within that structure there must rest a much more subjective and nuanced lens through which students can find individualized understanding and be guided into a particular type of thinking. Fixating on the verbs in the wheel or the rigor of the standards leads to the impression that teachers can create deep thought for their students. But the work has to be done in the students' minds as they examine texts or solve problems looking through individualized lenses at various DOK levels. We cannot teach a-ha moments, but we can facilitate them by providing lenses that are the right prescription for giving new vision to an individual student, within the structured frame we have created.

Challenge Questions:

1. Are you familiar with the image of the DOK word wheel?

2. Have you gotten stuck on the verbs rather than focusing on the cognitive processes behind them?

3. In what ways could DOK be a "frame" to provide structure?

4. In what ways could DOK be a "lens" to give new vision to students?

Discuss your responses with other teachers.

5. DIVING IN BEYOND THE WORD WHEEL: A METAPHOR

Have you ever heard of "blue holes"? They are deep underwater caves that, from the top, look like dark blue spots surrounded by shallow water or marshy land. But dive in, and you'll find they extend hundreds of feet, in one case over a thousand feet down, even branching out sideways into dark tunnels. These caves were once rock formations on land. Sea levels rose over time, filling the deepest parts of the caves with saltwater from the ground, while the surface levels are accumulated freshwater, like a lake. Because of this layering of water, the depths of some blue holes are devoid of oxygen, making them a perfect preservation chamber for fossils. These blue holes hold a wealth of information for those who are trained to dive in and explore (Kakuk, 2016).

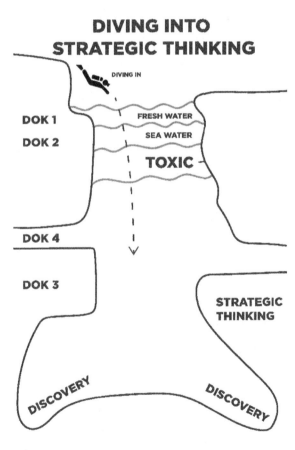

Teaching depth of knowledge levels 3 and 4 is like teaching how to stop swimming around at the surface and dive all the way down to the oxygen-free zone where new discoveries can be made. As they attempt to cross through watery layers to the anoxic depths, cave divers encounter a foggy layer of orange-tinted solution, called hydrogen sulfide. It is poisonous, seeping into the skin, so the divers must hurry through it to the clearer waters below.

As teachers and students, many of us are stuck at DOK level 2, the understanding level, teaching facts and figures. We have yet to break through the toxic fog to level 3. But we can't do that by simply instructing them to "think deeply," any more than an underwater dive instructor can simply say, "just dive in!" There are necessary tools and training. There is a process for facilitating deeper thought, and guiding them through that toxic layer will then give them the freedom to explore, invent, and solve problems they never thought they could.

Graphic by Christine Bursoto. Adapted from images at BahamasCaves.com

Challenge Questions:

1. Does the image of a diver exploring the depths give you a clearer understanding of the goals of DOK?

2. Look at the location of the DOK 4 label on the diagram on the previous page. Why do you think DOK 4 is placed in the horizontally extending passageways of the caves?

3. Can you identify any specific examples of your class struggling to break through the "toxic layer" into deeper thought? What was holding them back?

Discuss your responses with other teachers.

6. BREAKING THROUGH TO STRATEGIC THINKING

In this book we do not devote much space to levels 1 and 2 because most teachers are already masters at teaching the recall and understanding levels, and because we see a greater need for engaging on the deeper levels. Instead, this is a book about how to break through that toxic layer to levels 3 and 4, where there is so much untapped potential for learning.

What are the Toxic Barriers?

We have identified two categories of barriers to deep thinking that can form the "toxic level": barriers of classroom culture and barriers of skill and practice.

1. **Barriers of Classroom Culture** include such problems as...
    *   Lesson designs that misjudge the rigor level of the standards;
    *   Teacher roles that keep students from taking ownership of their learning; and
    *   An environment that limits participation or productive failure.

2. **Barriers of Skill and Practice** include such problems as...
    *   Students' lack of metacognition (thinking about their own thinking);
    *   Insufficient skills for organizing information and collaborating effectively;
    *   An imbalance between opportunities for effortful thinking work with opportunities for drawing on prior knowledge; and
    *   Misalignment of rigor between standards, formative assessments, and summative assessments.

Can you think of any elements of your classroom culture or your teaching practice that present barriers to deeper thinking?

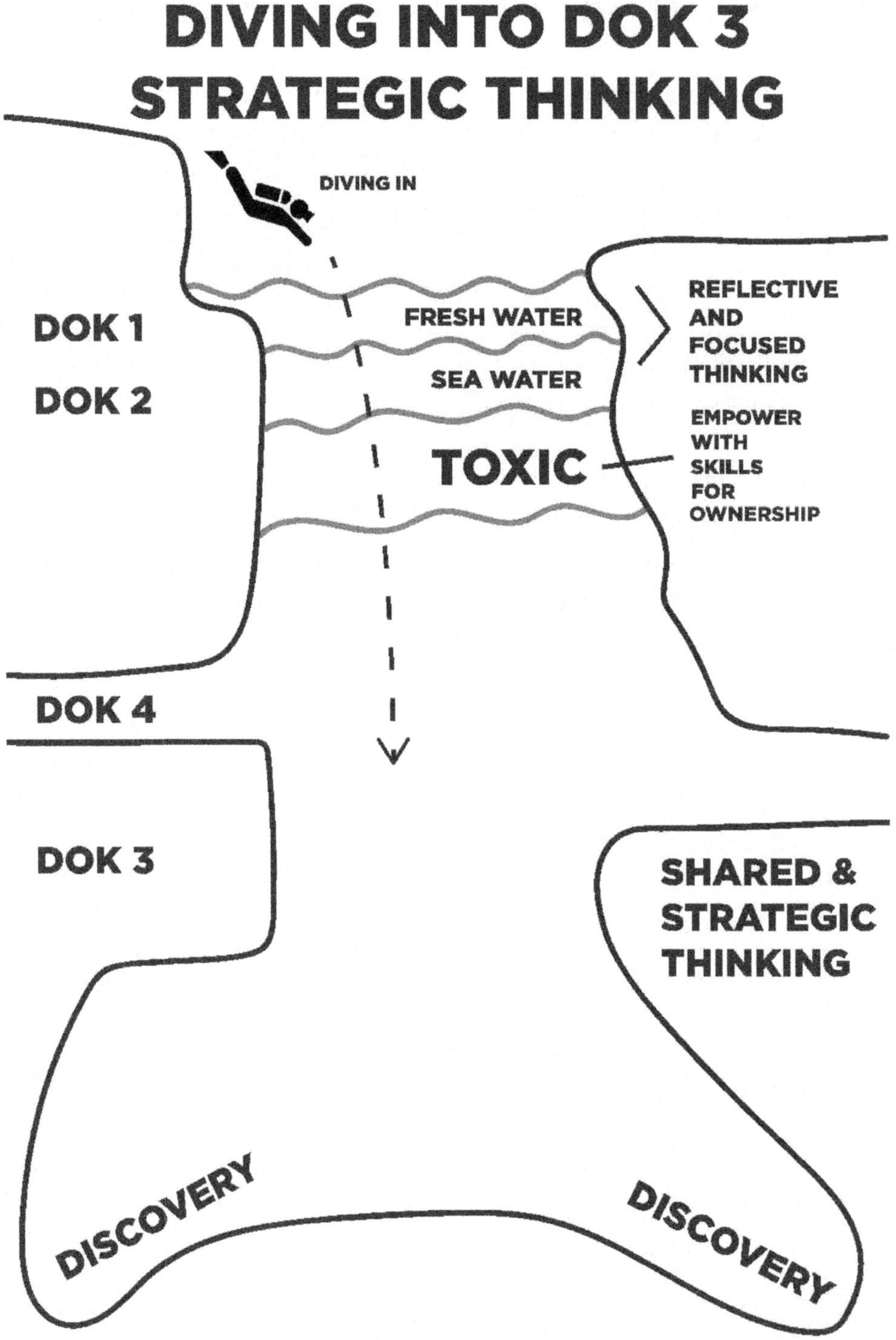
DIVING INTO DOK 3
STRATEGIC THINKING
DIVING IN
DOK 1
DOK 2
FRESH WATER
SEA WATER
TOXIC
REFLECTIVE
AND
FOCUSED
THINKING
EMPOWER
WITH
SKILLS
FOR
OWNERSHIP
DOK 4
DOK 3
SHARED &
STRATEGIC
THINKING
DISCOVERY
DISCOVERY

Here is a diagram of the blue hole with various types of thinking labeled on the right side.

A Process for Breaking Through

The facing page shows the blue hole diagram with four kinds of thinking labeled on the right side: **Reflective Thinking, Focused Thinking, Shared Thinking, Strategic Thinking.**

Have you ever considered engaging students in multiple thought processes as a strategy for reaching deeper thought? Write down any questions or ideas you may have about what reflective, focused, shared, and strategic thinking look like in practical terms.

To burst through the toxic layer, we need to approach the learning process differently, focusing not on the results or on the verbiage of our instructions, but on the cognitive processes of the learners. Our approach to this breakthrough involves the following process:

1. Students engage in **reflective thinking**, empowered by metacognitive skills to understand their own minds.
2. Students engage in **focused thinking**, empowered by skilled systems for organizing their thoughts.
3. Students engage in **shared thinking**, collaborating effectively because of the reflection and focus they have done, and empowered by learned collaborative norms. The teacher facilitates equitable productive talk. *Note: It is entirely possible to reach strategic thinking without collaboration, but we believe everyone's best strategic thinking is refined by others.*
4. Students repeat the above reflective and focused thinking individually, this time evaluating information through the new lenses gained in collaboration or through the reading of multiple related texts or perspectives. The result is **strategic thinking**.

Parts 2 and 3 of this book will detail the necessary classroom culture and practical skills for helping students to progress through this thinking process, breaking through the toxic barriers.

Challenge: Identify Toxic Barriers #1

Check out the following poetry lesson. As you read through it, see if you can identify the barriers that might keep students from entering strategic thinking. Below this section you'll find this complete lesson with instructions for using it effectively and breaking through these barriers.

> *Eighth grade students in Mrs. Suchandsuch's class are working on a poetry unit. She intends for students to meet the following Common Core State Standard ELA-LITERACY.RL.8.4:*
>
> *Determine the meaning of words and phrases as they are used in a text, including figurative and connotative meanings; analyze the impact of specific word choices on meaning and tone, including analogies or allusions to other texts.*
>
> *She hands out a translated Old English poem called "The Anchor" and then she waits a few minutes while students read it quietly to themselves. She calls on volunteers to discuss how the title is literal but the poem seems to be figurative. She asks, "What do you think the anchor is? Is it a person, place, or thing?" She continues asking students thinking questions about the author's word choice. Following a Q&A session, Mrs. Suchandsuch defines the words tone, analogy, and allusion. Then the students reread the poem to find examples of these three literary devices. She leads the class in a think-pair-share, discussing the examples they found and writing them on the whiteboard. Finally, students write a paragraph about their perceptions of the poem's meaning.*

On the following pages you'll find a strategy for teaching this lesson that contrasts with Mrs. Suchandsuch's approach. We have included the complete lesson with instructions for making it a DOK 3 lesson by bringing them through the process we've described: reflective, focused, and shared thinking. *(Standard retrieved from CCSSI, 2016)*

The Anchor Poetry Lesson: A Strategic Thinking Approach

Mrs. Suchandsuch's approach to this lesson could be improved by moving students through reflective, focused, and shared thinking, allowing them to reach strategic thinking.

Common Core State Standard ELA-LITERACY.RL.8.4:

Determine the meaning of words and phrases as they are used in a text, including figurative and connotative meanings; analyze the impact of specific word choices on meaning and tone, including analogies or allusions to other texts.
(Retrieved from CCSSI, 2016)

REFLECTIVE THINKING

- Prompt students' interest with a Big Idea posted in the room, "Authors craft their words to manipulate our thoughts."
- Engage students to respond to this Big Idea with an elbow partner exercise so that each student thinks and talks about the topic. Limit this to just a couple of minutes.
- Ask students for examples from lyrics, poems, and advertisements of how artists and marketers deliberately shape thinking. Students may find song lyrics and advertisements to be particularly relevant and interesting.

FOCUSED THINKING

- Pass out a copy of the poem (next page) to students, omitting the title. Ask them to listen and follow along as you read for fluency.
- Next, ask students to read the poem a second time to themselves while annotating, using your class's established annotation system (see module 17). You can choose to have them focus on any part of the annotation anchor chart, or specific areas, depending on your standard objective.

Poetry Title: _____?

Sometimes I travel along under The waves,

where no one can see me,

hunting The bottom of the ocean.

The sea whips And heaves, tossing up whitened foam,

Roaring and shrieking,

Flooding water Crashes and beats on the shore,

hurling Stones and sand and seaweed and great breaking Waves on the

high cliffs, while I go struggling deep in the ocean, thrashing in its

darkness.

But I can't escape,

pull off the waves from my back, till He allows me He who always guides

me, Say…Wise man,

who draws me from the ocean's arms when the waters are still again,

when the waves that covered me over are gentle and calm.

(Source: Olsen, 1998)

SHARED THINKING (Breaking through the toxic barrier)

- Use an adapted version of think-pair-share, called The Carousel (see module 11 for instructions), for collaboration. This will allow for equitable instruction, where every student talks productively about every prompt. We have included prompts on the following page that you can use for this activity.

- We recommend grouping students in threes so that each student feels some responsibility to speak (you may need to add additional prompts to allow for smaller groups).

- Instruct students to bring their poetry text when they rotate around the room to the various prompts posted on the walls. Instruct them in the carousel process of writing and responding to ideas on the prompt paper (see module 11 for details).

- Model to students the use of evidence in answering the prompts. For example, with Prompt #1, you might write on the chart paper, "A Plea for Help" as a possible title, drawing a line connecting it to the evidence phrase "…pull off the waves from my back…"

- Encourage the group members to paraphrase each other. Before writing a member's idea, someone else should clarify the thought: "So what I think you mean is…" Clarity allows for effective collaboration.

32

> **Open-Ended Prompts**
>
> Prompt #1: What would you use as the title of this poem? Support your choice with evidence from the text.
>
> Prompt #2: Which literary techniques does the author use? Cite examples with your choices.
>
> Prompt #3: What are the context clues the author uses to clue us in on what the poem is about? Give examples when you can.
>
> Prompt #4: What is the purpose to the line "But I can't escape"? How did you make this inference?
>
> Prompt #5: How does the author deliberately direct our thinking? Give specific evidence.

STRATEGIC THINKING

- Go over all the carousel responses as a class. Have teams defend their posts to the class and use the Fishbowl prompts (module 9) to ask probing questions. Save the prompt about the title until the end.

- Have students take 2-column Cornell Notes (see module 13), categorizing them using key words from the academic standard: *figurative, connotative, word choice, analogy, allusion*. Lead a discussion of literal versus figurative, since most students tend to think figuratively with this poem selection.

- Next, challenge them through "forced agreement" to choose the best title, with a supporting "why" to defend the choice. Then explain that the title of the poem is "The Anchor."

- Read the poem again, now that they know the title, and ask students if the title changes their understanding.

EXTENDED STRATEGIC THINKING (DOK 4)

- Use part 2 of the problem-solving frame that follows, with the "problem" being, "Find symbols that are nearly interchangeable with *anchor* in poetry."

- Challenge students to search the Internet for 4 other poems with "anchor" in the title. They should then work on problem-solving frames independently, providing textual evidence for their answers. This step could be completed as a think-pair-share.

- Facilitate a conversation about the types of thinking they relied upon to complete the problem-solving frame (analytical, creative, etc.)

- Encourage students to write a poem that follows the model of *The Anchor (Problem-solving frame source: Cash, 2011).*

Problem-Solving Frame Part 1

What's Your PROBLEM?

Possible Cause #1	**Cause:** *What's your evidence? How do you back this claim up?* * *
Possible Cause #2	**Cause:** *What's your evidence? How do you back this claim up?* * *
Possible Cause #3	**Cause:** *What's your evidence? How do you back this claim up?* * *

What's Your PROBLEM?

Can you support the best possible solution?

Possible Solution #1	Possible Solution: Evidence to Support: 1. 2.
Possible Solution #2	Possible Solution: Evidence to Support: 1. 2.
Possible Solution #3	Possible Solution: Evidence to Support: 1. 2.

GROUP AGREEMENT!

Challenge: Identify Toxic Barriers #2

Here is Mrs. Suchandsuch again. Now she's teaching a lesson on argumentative writing. This time, we have included a list of barriers that we identified at the end of the lesson.

Eighth grade students file into their English Language Arts classroom and take their seats facing the front of the room. Their teacher, Mrs. Suchandsuch, has written a "Big Idea" on the board: "Kids who frequently play violent video games have a greater tendency to become more violent and aggressive than non-video game players." Several boys roll their eyes.

Mrs. Suchandsuch intends for her students to reach the Common Core State Standard W.8.1., writing an argument and supporting a claim with clear reasons and relevant evidence. She begins class by reading the Big Idea, and showing a PowerPoint of various pro and con arguments. She reads each statement aloud, pausing to point out claims, counterclaims, reasons, and evidence. A few students list these terms in their notebooks, and the rest seem to be listening. One student raises her hand to disagree with one of the written statements and says it is a weak argument, so Mrs. Suchandsuch asks the girl whether or not it has evidence. She explains to her students that an argument can be strong even if you disagree with it and asks the girl to find another statement she disagrees with but still finds to be a strong argument. She picks out a couple more statements and asks for volunteers to point out their evidence and categorize them as "strong" or "weak."

Mrs. Suchandsuch then writes three controversial statements on the board. For homework students are to choose one and write a three paragraph essay arguing for or against the statement, being sure to include clear claims, counterclaims, reasons, and evidence. The completed essays will be her benchmark for assessing how well students understand argumentative writing.

On the following pages you'll find a list of toxic barriers that we identified in Mrs. Suchandsuch's lesson. You'll also find a strategy for teaching this lesson that contrasts with Mrs. Suchandsuch's approach.

Toxic Barriers
Argumentative Writing Lesson

1. No collaboration—students are not encouraged to debate the topic or share their perspectives. The physical classroom setup does not place students in close proximity to each other to encourage inclusive sharing of ideas.

2. Lacking autonomy—the lesson is teacher-driven, with students participating only when called upon.

3. Lack of reflective thinking—except for the girl who is asked to find an argument she disagrees with that is still a strong argument, students do not reflect on their own thought process to determine how they came to their conclusions. This could have been improved by having students debate the topic, recording their arguments and then labeling and evaluating each other's statements.

4. Lack of skills for focused thinking—a few students try to take notes, but they do not have the skills for organizing the information effectively. Most students listen but do not follow any purposeful method for making the information their own.

5. A focus on outcome—Mrs. Suchandsuch does not assess her students' understanding of the concepts until she has read their essays. Rather than embedding formative assessments as she guides them through the thought process, she is focusing on the outcome.

6. Lack of anchoring and multiplicity—the lesson begins and ends with this one topic, and it does not give students a chance to see the structure of logical arguments through their own experience. Although they read through several statements, they do not analyze any other complex types of argument, such as song, poetry, or political cartoon, from which they would need to infer claims, reasons, and evidence.

7. Lack of time extension—this lesson took 1 day, so there wasn't sufficient time to draw students into deep thinking or creative practice.

Challenge: Revise The Lesson for Mrs. Suchandsuch

Help a teacher out! After identifying the barriers Mrs. Suchandsuch faced, help her to revise her lesson plan so her students can think strategically. Incorporate the following elements into your plan:

- Lesson broken into 5 distinguishable parts
    1. Identifying claims/evidence
    2. Evaluating strength of arguments
    3. Detecting bias
    4. Identifying counterarguments
    5. Making inferences/drawing conclusions
- Collaboration that doesn't give anyone an "out"
- Mrs. Suchandsuch modeling her thinking
- Use of a graphic organizer
- Use of cards printed with pro/con arguments to pass out for group work (sample arguments are on the following pages)
- Allows students to engage their own opinions through debate

PRO ARGUMENTS (for use with revised lesson)

Violent video games contribute to youth violence

- Increasing reports of bullying can be partially attributed to the popularity of violent video games. The 2008 study *Grand Theft Childhood* reported that 60% of middle school boys who played at least one Mature-rated game hit or beat up someone, compared to 39% of boys that did not play Mature-rated games.
- Video games often reward players for simulating violence, and thus enhance the learning of violent behaviors. Studies suggest that when violence is rewarded in video games, players exhibit increased aggressive behavior compared to players of video games where violence is punished.
- Violent video games desensitize players to real-life violence. It is common for victims in video games to disappear off screen when they are killed or for players to have multiple lives. In a 2005 study, violent video game exposure has been linked to reduced P300 amplitudes in the brain, which is associated with desensitization to violence and increases in aggressive behavior.
- A 2000 FBI report includes playing violent video games in a list of behaviors associated with school shootings.

- Violent video games teach youth that violence is an acceptable conflict-solving strategy and an appropriate way to achieve one's goals. A 2009 study found that youth who play violent video games have lower belief in the use of nonviolent strategies and are less forgiving than players of nonviolent video games.

- Violent video games cause players to associate pleasure and happiness with the ability to cause pain in others.

- Young children are more likely to confuse fantasy violence with real world violence, and without a framework for ethical decision-making, they may mimic the actions they see in violent video games.

- Violent video games require active participation, repetition, and identification with the violent character. With new game controllers allowing more physical interaction, the immersive and interactive characteristics of video games can increase the likelihood of youth violence.

- Playing violent video games increases aggressive behavior and arousal. A 2009 study found that it takes up to four minutes for the level of aggressive thoughts and feelings in children to return to normal after playing violent video games. It takes five to ten minutes for heart rate and aggressive behavior to return to baseline. Video games that show the most blood generate more aggressive thoughts. When blood is present in video games, there is a measurable increase in arousal and hostility.

- Playing violent video games causes the development of aggressive behavioral scripts. A behavioral script is developed from the repetition of actions and affects the subconscious mind. An example of a common behavioral script is a driving script that tells drivers to get in a vehicle, put on a seat belt, and turn on the ignition. Similarly, violent video games can lead to scripts that tell youth to respond aggressively in certain situations. Violence in video games may lead to real world violence when scripts are automatically triggered in daily life, such as being nudged in a school hallway.

- A 1998 study found that 21% of games sampled involved violence against women. Exposure to sexual violence in video games is linked to increases in violence towards women and false attitudes about rape such as that women incite men to rape or that women secretly desire rape.

- Several studies in both the United States and Japan have shown that, controlling for prior aggression, children who played more violent video games during the beginning of the school year showed more aggression than their peers later in the school year.

- Exposure to violent video games is linked to lower empathy in players. In a 2004 study of 150 fourth and fifth graders by Professor Jeanne Funk, violent video games were the only type of media associated with lower empathy. Empathy, the ability to understand and enter into another's feelings, plays an important role in the process of moral evaluation and is believed to inhibit aggressive behavior.

CON ARGUMENTS (for use with revised lesson)

Violent video games contribute to youth violence.

- Violent juvenile crime in the United States has been declining as violent video game popularity has increased. The arrest rate for juvenile murders has fallen 71.9% between 1995 and 2008. The arrest rate for all juvenile violent crimes has declined 49.3%. In this same period, video game sales have more than quadrupled.

- A causal link between violent video games and violent behavior has not been proven. Many studies suffer from design flaws and use unreliable measures of violence and aggression such as noise blast tests. Thoughts about aggression have been confused with aggressive behavior, and there is a lack of studies that follow children over long periods of time.

- A 2004 US Secret Service review of previous school-based attacks found that one-eighth of attackers exhibited an interest in violent video games, less than the rate of interest attackers showed in violent movies, books, and violence in their own writings. The report did not find a relationship between playing violent video games and school shootings.

- The small correlations that have been found between video games and violence may be explained by violent youth being drawn to violent video games. Violent games do not cause youth to be violent. Instead, youth that are predisposed to be violent seek out violent entertainment such as video games.

- Playing violent video games reduces violence in adolescent boys by serving as a substitute for rough and tumble play. Playing violent video games allows adolescent boys to express aggression and establish status in the peer group without causing physical harm.

- Video game players understand they are playing a game. Their ability to distinguish between fantasy and reality prevents them from emulating video game violence in real life.

- Playing violent video games provides a safe outlet for aggressive and angry feelings. A 2007 study reported that 45% of boys played video games because "it helps me get my anger out" and 62% played because it "helps me relax."

- Violent video games provide healthy and safe opportunities for children to virtually explore rules and consequences of violent actions. Violent games also allow youth to experiment with issues such as war, violence and death without real world consequences.

- The level of control granted to video game players, especially in terms of pace and directing the actions of their character, allows youth to regulate their emotional state during play. Research shows that a perception of being in control reduces emotional and stressful responses to events.

- Alarmist claims similar to current arguments against violent video games have been made in the past when new media such as radio, movies, and television have been introduced. Claims that these various mediums would result in surges in youth violence also failed to materialize.

- Violent video games may affect the form of violence, but they do not cause the violence to occur. Youth might model violent acts on what they have seen in video games, but the violence would still occur in the absence of video games.

- Exposure to violent video games has not been shown to be predictive of violent behavior or crime. Any link found between video games and violence is best explained by other variables such as exposure to family violence and aggressive personality.

- When research does show that violent video games cause more arousal and aggression, it is because the comparative game is less exciting. A short-term increase in arousal and aggression does not mean a child is going to leave his or her house and commit a violent act.

- In 2005, the US had 2,279 murders committed by teenagers (27.9 per million residents) compared to 73 in Japan (3.1 per million). Per capita video game sales were $5.20 in the US compared to $47 in Japan. This example illustrates that there is no correlation between violent behavior and playing video games.

Challenge Questions:

1. Can you identify some of the barriers that keep your students from breaking through to deeper levels of thought?

2. Think of activities and strategies you currently use to bring your students into different cognitive tasks. List them under the heading where they fit best:

> Reflective Thinking

> Focused Thinking

> Shared Thinking

> Strategic Thinking

Discuss your responses with other teachers.

PART 1 TAKEAWAYS

- Depth of Knowledge is not linear: all types of thought are necessary parts of a whole.
- Depth of Knowledge is not about verbs used to instruct. The verbs are the result, not the way to get there.
- A "toxic" barrier exists that keeps many classrooms operating at levels 1 and 2.
- DOK 1 (recall) and DOK 2 (concept) are taught very well in today's classrooms, while DOK 3 and 4 are often harder to reach and harder to measure.
- DOK 3 (strategic thinking) is about making new connections in the brain: figuring out how to solve a problem, recognizing evidence, evaluating what makes an answer the BEST answer out of many good answers
- DOK 4 (extended thinking) is not necessarily harder than DOK 3. It is simply longer or wider. It makes connections in a new context or over a long period of time.

List additional takeaways below.

2
PREPARE FOR EXPLORATION

This section of the book describes the classroom environment and general approach that is necessary for DOK 3 and 4. Your teaching style and classroom culture must be conducive to those levels of student thought. Part 2 will help you hone your style so you can get the most out of the practical lessons in Part 3.

In This Section

7. Setting the Stage: The Importance of Classroom Environment
8. Identify Your Standards by DOK Level
9. Adjust for Complexity
10. Grant Autonomy
11. Leverage Peer Feedback
12. Embrace Failure
13. Focus on Process, Not Outcome
14. Tips for High Ability Students

Where do I stand?

❑   I think my current classroom culture will be conducive to strategic thinking.

❑   I could improve the culture of my classroom, but I'm not sure where to start.

❑   I give my students autonomy, but they can't seem to collaborate effectively.

❑   My students prefer giving easy answers to sharing original thoughts because they are afraid of failure.

❑   My students are preoccupied with grades and don't appreciate the value of learning.

❑   I know how to create the right classroom culture, but I struggle to find time for deeper thinking activities.

❑   I use data to align my formative assessments with summative assessments.

❑   I have a successful DOK 3-4 activity or idea I can share.

Discuss your responses with other teachers.

---

7. SETTING THE STAGE:
THE IMPORTANCE OF CLASSROOM ENVIRONMENT

Creating a classroom that supports thought at levels 3 and 4 will require some planning. The environment and culture of your classroom will be the fertile soil in which the practical skills in Part 3 can take root.

Think like a Marketer

You know the principle of product placement: junk food placed at eye level sells faster than sweets that are out of sight. Treadmills in family rooms stand a better chance at being used than those in the basement. And deep thinking occurs more readily in classrooms that promote it in their culture and environment. If strategic thinking comes from skillful reflection and focus combined with effective shared thinking, we must place that process within arm's reach of our students, by planning an intentional classroom environment.

The skills that will lead most effectively to strategic thinking—skills for pushing through a process of reflection, focus, and collaboration—are noncognitive skills like self-control and grit. In fact, IQ has very little to do with how deeply a student is willing to think (Stanovich, 2009). Qualities like perseverance and curiosity and conscientiousness are more important to success in intensive thinking work. And so it is vital to help students develop these character qualities. But they are more easily absorbed than taught. Overt efforts to teach and measure noncognitive skills don't usually work (Tough, 2016). It is most effective to place these noncognitive skills on the shelf at eye level than to sing their praises. That means creating a classroom environment—both physical and cultural—that allows the deep thinking process to happen more naturally.

> ## Check This Out!
> For a more in-depth discussion of how to create a classroom environment where noncognitive skills like grit flourish, we recommend Paul Tough's *Helping Children Succeed: What Works and Why* (Houghton Mifflin Harcourt, 2016).

The Intentional Environment

"How do I feel?" is one of the key questions students subconsciously ask themselves before learning can take place (Marzano, 2010). Set up the physical space so that students feel like they belong and can contribute. For DOK 3-4 class discussions, place desks in a circle or in groups of 3, so students face each other rather than the teacher, and no one is behind anyone else. Physical proximity is a powerful tool for enabling collaboration. Students are more likely to invest personally—asking questions, sharing ideas, and in general acting "gritty"—when they are physically positioned in a manner that suggests safety, equality, and inclusion.

IQ has little to do with how deeply a student will think.

Position your students and yourself so that you can nudge students into deeper thinking. Teachers should be conscious of the less-obvious factors of the classroom environment that affect students' DOK 3 and 4 thinking opportunities. A teacher who is "with it" at DOK 3 and 4 understands the DOK level of specific academic standards, facilitates peer conversations to help make them effective, and appreciates the student's thought process. Awareness of subtleties—like perceiving that someone is about to shut down someone else's idea, or knowing the just-right level of complexity for an individual student—sets the tone for a classroom's culture.

This "with-it"-ness is more an art than a science. Nonetheless, we have identified six specific actions you can take to eliminate "toxic barriers" to strategic thinking associated with classroom culture:

- Identify DOK Standards
- Adjust for Complexity
- Grant autonomy
- Leverage peer feedback
- Focus on process over outcome
- Embrace failure

Throughout the rest of Part 2, we will examine each of these aspects of classroom culture in detail, with examples of techniques you can use to bring each aspect into your classroom.

Safe Sharing Technique: The 30-Second Talkabout

A quick, simple method to coax out collaboration with an emphasis on making students feel safe enough to share their ideas.

The technique: Students stand up and partner up, facing each other with one assigned the role of "talker" and the other the role of "listener." Partners take turns in these roles, each challenged to say as much as they can on an assigned topic for 30 seconds without stopping or getting off topic. After everyone has been both a "talker" and a "listener" the teacher calls on students to summarize what their partner had said as "talker."

Remember: For a good talkabout, the teacher must walk about!

When to use it: Since it only takes a few minutes and no supplies, the 30-second talkabout can be used anytime, but it's especially helpful as a quick way to keep students engaged in the middle of a lesson or lecture, and especially during larger class discussions in which only outspoken students have willingly engaged.

Why it works: Students are out of their seats, engaging kinesthetic learning styles. Talking is done one-on-one, so it's less intimidating. Having to say as much as possible in a short amount of time brings an element of fun and competitiveness, breaking down students' inhibitions. And when the teacher calls on students, they don't share their own ideas with the class. They share their partner's ideas, which is less daunting. The 30-second talkabout engages every single student productively in a relaxed environment.

What are some other activities you can use that engage multiple learning styles, break down inhibitions, and make students feel safe to share?

Challenge Questions:

1. To what extent do you think character qualities like grit and conscientiousness can be consciously "taught"? To what extent do they depend on the classroom environment?

2. Have you thought about the importance of classroom culture in making deeper thinking possible?

Discuss your responses with other teachers.

8. IDENTIFY YOUR STANDARDS BY DOK LEVEL

Look at lessons, standards, and test questions through the lens of DOK.

The environment you create for your classroom—not just the physical environment, but the culture, the teaching style, the pace—should be fluid, changing to accommodate the lesson you are teaching. A DOK 1 lesson should look much different from a DOK 3 lesson, and so forth. In preparing any lesson, teachers identify the academic standards that are to be taught. We suggest that you go one step further and identify the DOK levels that you want your students to reach during the lesson.

Decoding Rigor

We recommend the "backward design" of standards-based education, with a specific focus on DOK. You may have heard the popular phrase "begin with the end in mind" (Covey, 1989). To some teachers, that phrase leaves a bad taste because it sounds like "teach to the test" or "focus on outcomes." But it is a morally neutral phrase that can be a useful approach when done right. What matters is what your "end" is. If your "end" is the learning itself, it certainly should be your beginning, and your middle too.

If your "end" is dynamic lessons that promote lifelong learning and thinking skills, it helps to view everything—individual lessons, academic standards, and even standardized test questions—through the lens of DOK. It is possible, and quite helpful, to use standards and test questions as tools without making them your "end." The rigor that will lead to learning is subjective: it does not come automatically from using tougher standards. Instead rigor comes from how standards are applied to meet individual student needs, and using DOK can help with this. Look at your academic standards like they are code words, each one communicating a different DOK level.

Look at standardized test questions like they are your decoder ring, the missing piece that can tell you what the academic standard is trying to say about DOK. After you've cracked the code, you can structure each lesson according to the type of thinking its standard is really calling for, confident that your students will learn the material to the depth that the writers of the standard intended, and the level of likely test questions.

Let's practice the secret agent decoding process. On the facing page there is a sample Common Core State Standard from grade 8 English Language Arts. This is the same standard we shared back in Module 3.

Academic Standard Decoding Practice

CCSS.ELA-LITERACY.RL9-10.4
Determine the meaning of words and phrases as they are used in the text, including figurative and connotative meanings; analyze the cumulative impact of specific word choices on meaning and tone (e.g., how the language evokes a sense of time and place; how it sets a formal or informal tone) (CCSSI, 2016).

Here is a test question from a text about immigration that corresponds to the above standard.

> *Which of the following statements BEST describes the author's purpose for including the section "Just One Plan" in the above article?*
>
> A.   *To show that Abulateef will do whatever it takes to stay in the United States*
> B.   *To describe the long process and red tape that Iraqis must go through to stay in the United States*
> C.   *To provide context to for understanding the plight of displaced immigrants who, despite the efforts of attorneys, are unsafe in Iraq but illegal in the United States*
> D.   *To explain the goal of the asylum program*

Now here's how to deconstruct the standard and determine its DOK level. This process was originated by Shauna Finlay and Amy Leeson (Finlay, 2014).

1. *Underline the nouns and noun phrases in the standard to identify key concepts.*
2. *Circle the verbs to identify skills (circle the underlined nouns that will also require action, i.e. analysis for analyze).*
3. *Highlight key academic or domain-specific words.*
4. *Identify the securely held content from previous grade levels.*
5. *List skills required that are essential for proficiency.*
6. *Review your list of skills, and determine the DOK level necessary for each one. The highest DOK level included will be considered the DOK level of the standard.*
7. *Organize the learning targets (necessary skills) into a progression for that makes sense for instruction. Start by asking, "How will students make meaning for themselves?"*

You can see that the DOK level for this standard is level 3, strategic thinking. So in designing a lesson around it, you'll want to adjust your approach to give students the opportunity to think strategically. (That adjusting is what the rest of this book will show you how to do!)

To help you take your standards-based lesson designs to the next level, we have provided a sample curriculum map that takes DOK level into account.

Model Curriculum Map-DOK

Unit Title: _____

Unit Length: _____

Standards/ Benchmarks *State-tested*	DOK Level	Implications for Instruction (Content, Skills, Practice, Expected Rigor, Feedback Model, FITS)	Assessment Design (Securely Held Content & Skills)	Possible Real-World Connections, Audience, Authenticity, Connections to previous learning &/or other disciplines

Data Collected on Summative Assessment:

How we interpreted the Data:

Notes on Needed Revisions:

Next Steps for Teacher Leaders

Use the curriculum map on the previous page to lead other teachers toward a DOK-aware classroom. Collaborate with other teachers in your school to keep a focus on DOK and ensure opportunities for strategic thinking in all subjects and grade levels.

1. Work together to design instructional strategies and formative assessments, with attention to the DOK Level of standards.

2. Work together to create rubrics that measure how well a student takes ownership of the learning and engages in effortful thinking work.

3. Conduct conversations about vertical alignment with teachers of other grade levels to find "knowing-doing" gaps, overlaps, and holes in DOK levels of instruction.

4. Examine curriculum to continue to remove barriers by clarifying and confronting assumptions about learning, learners, and professional learning. Pay particular attention to teacher-student roles.

5. Analyze student work collaboratively and design weekly conversations around monitoring and tracking student learning, using DOK levels as a common language for discussing their progress.

6. Encourage colleagues to keep the thought process in mind when developing a grading system and when reporting progress to parents, rather than simply talking about outcomes.

7. Treat curriculum mapping as an ongoing "living process." Curriculum mapping should foster professional collaboration, growth, and change in teacher practice.

Post It

When you've identified the DOK levels you hope for your students to reach in a given lesson, it's a good idea to communicate that goal to your students, just as you might post the academic standard on the wall. You don't necessarily have to teach them the number or the term "depth of knowledge," but explain the kind of thinking you want them to do. Teaching them to think about how they think (see module 16 on metacognition) is part of the DOK 3-4 process. You may even find it helpful to use our blue hole metaphor (see module 5) to explain your goals to students.

Identify by DOK as a Time Management Tool

If you often feel you have too much too cover in too little time, use DOK to help you prioritize your time. Designing your lessons by decoding the academic standards can help you use your class time more efficiently. It would be pointless to design performance tasks that take a lot of time if they are only aligned to DOK level 1 or 2 standards. Viewing the planning process through the lens of DOK allows you to align the rigor—and time intensity—of your lessons to the rigor of the standards, so you get the most out of your teaching time.

Challenge Questions:

1. Does a desire not to "teach to the test" keep you from using standards and test questions as a tool for real learning?

2. Does your teaching and planning change from lesson to lesson, depending on how deeply you want your students to think?

3. How could you use the DOK lens to make better use of your instructional time?

Discuss your responses with other teachers.

9. ADJUST FOR COMPLEXITY

Once you have identified the DOK level of the standards for a lesson (module 8), you'll need to adjust your approach to a given lesson accordingly.

Spiral Complexity

Try to spiral complexity from lesson to lesson, spacing out lessons that are DOK 3 and 4 with some DOK 1 and 2 lessons in between. Remember, level 3 is not always harder than level 2, but it is necessarily more complex, requiring more involved thought processes. Even within a single lesson it can be helpful to vary the types of thinking required. Periods of less-complex activity give the more complicated ideas time to sink in. Move between the four levels of thinking to ensure that you activate all levels of thought and achieve wholeness in learning. Take a cue from the standardized test questions (a.k.a. Decoders-see module 8). Text-dependent questions that demand strategic thinking tend to spiral in complexity. So to teach strategic thinking in your class, use the same strategy.

Plan for a Multi-Step Approach

When you skim the surface levels, it's easy to cover a lot of area, but probing the depths takes more time. Allot a bit more time for DOK 3 lessons, and even more time for DOK 4 (see module 21). Strategic and extended thinking require the time for taking multiple exploratory ventures into a single topic to understand it better.

Underwater cave divers don't just dive in and immediately explore the depths. They make multiple dives into the same blue hole. Their first dive, called a "shakedown" dive, helps them to understand the layout of the cave, take stock of any possible hazards, and take lots of photos so they can plan for their next dive (PBS Nova, 2013). Similarly, students need a multi-step approach to deeper thought. Remember these steps from Part 1? Keep them in mind as you plan.

1. Students engage in **reflective thinking**, empowered by metacognitive skills to understand their own minds.
2. Students engage in **focused thinking**, empowered by skilled systems for organizing their thoughts.
3. Students engage in **shared thinking**, collaborating effectively because of the reflection and focus they have done, and empowered by learned collaborative norms. *Note: It is entirely possible to reach strategic thinking without collaboration, but we believe everyone's best strategic thinking is refined by others.*
4. Students repeat the above reflective and focused thinking individually, this time evaluating information through the new lenses gained in collaboration or through the reading of multiple related texts or perspectives. The result is **strategic thinking**.

Choosing Complex Text

A 2006 report released by ACT, Inc., revealed data showing that students were disproportionately missing questions that are based on complex texts. So when students did not achieve a "benchmark" on the ACT Reading Test, the cause was less likely to be a lack of academic skills in general and more likely to be an inability to read and understand complex text in particular. Over the next several years, "text complexity" would become a big deal for teachers.

But what exactly does "complexity" mean? It's not quite the same as "difficulty." Identifying it requires more than simply asking, "Can my students read at this level?" The ACT determines the complexity of a text by looking at six aspects of the text and determining whether each aspect is straightforward or intricate:

1. **Relationships** (interactions among ideas or characters)
2. **Richness** (amount and sophistication of information conveyed through data or literary devices)
3. **Structure** (how the text is organized and how it progresses)
4. **Style** (author's tone and use of language)
5. **Vocabulary** (author's word choice)
6. **Purpose** (author's intent in writing the text)
   (ACT, 2006)

If you choose texts for your students based only on "difficulty," or by simply getting a feel for complexity when you read through it, consider adopting a more procedural approach. When you're looking for complex texts to use in your classroom, think through the above six aspects. Look for texts that contain the following:

1. Subtle or deeply embedded relationships between ideas
2. Richness in data or details
3. Elaborate or unconventional organization
4. Intricate style or unexpected tone
5. A context-dependent vocabulary
6. An implied or ambiguous purpose

Allow for Reach and Reciprocity

Divers in the Bahamas found the skull of a crocodile from thousands of years ago. In the same underwater cave they found a tortoise shell. Back on land, later, they looked over their findings and noticed that bite marks on the tortoise shell matched up perfectly with the measurements of the crocodile's teeth. Then they understood that the two separate findings were connected: the crocodile must have gone into the blue hole in pursuit of the tortoise, and then after eating it was unable to get out of the steep-sided hole, where it has been preserved for centuries. (PBS, 2013).

When we learn, we start with what we already know, then we dive in and discover something new that we can connect to our prior knowledge. Then we come back to the surface, reflect and organize our findings, and dive in again later to find more. It isn't until we've returned to the surface a second time that we can see both of our new discoveries side-by-side and begin to understand their relationship. Making this connection, this eureka moment, can sometimes happen during the active thinking time, while we are exploring the underwater caves, but it more often happens in the downtime just after we've surfaced from the depths of our conscious thought.

Richard Ogle calls the exploring of new ideas "reach." For learning, reach must be balanced with "reciprocity," which is the coming back to the surface, the re-organizing of what we thought we knew before through the lens of our new discoveries (Ogle, 2007).

> ### Resources For Finding Complex Text
>
> **Engage NY**
> EngageNY.org – Features full lessons you can download for free that are completely aligned to complex texts and text dependent questions.
>
> **Newsela**
> Newsela.com – Updated weekly with relevant stories on current events and interesting articles. Features a quiz option for teachers for each text. Best of all, each text can be manipulated according to the student's Lexile level.
>
> **EL Education**
> https://vimeo.com/54007714 - A seven-minute video of a 5th grade class engaging in close reading with complex text.

We can't "teach" those eureka moments, but we can create the ideal space for them to pop up. New information needs incubation time, so break complex thinking lessons into parts to allow time for coming back up to the surface to reflect between reading texts. Move on to something tangential for a little while, something that seems unrelated but might share a connecting link. Spread a DOK 4 lesson out over a number of days or weeks, allowing the brain to use those non-school hours, and especially nights of sleep, to work its own magic. Many scientists believe that during sleep the brain is working to organize and reinforce the things that have been learned during the day (Brooks, 2011). Perhaps spreading lessons out, rather than cramming more in, could, counterintuitively, be a more efficient use of our time.

What is one lesson you currently use that you could break into chunks and space out over a day, week, or weeks? How could spacing it out allow you to add supplemental complex texts? Use this space to brainstorm ideas.

Over the next several pages you'll find a practical lesson strategy that is especially good for allowing students to approach a topic from multiple angles and allowing for both reach and reciprocity.

Multi-Step Lesson: The Declaration of Independence

Consider the following multi-step approach to reading the Declaration of Independence, a primary text that many students might find dry with a more traditional approach. Underlined activities are explained in detail on the following pages.

Step 1: Use the 5 Whys activity (details to follow) as a pre-reading primer to activate students' prior knowledge and get them thinking before reading the text. Start with a statement: The colonists want to break free from Great Britain. Then have students work backwards to determine cause-effect relationships on why the colonists want independence. Spend just a few minutes on this activity to see how far they get.

Step 2: Read the Declaration of Independence aloud for students, modeling for fluency. Since this is a difficult primary text, teacher modeling is helpful. You can break the text down and read one paragraph at a time, alternating between step 2 and step 3 below.

Step 3: Have students read a second time through the text that they just heard you read aloud. Challenge the students to annotate text as they read individually (see module 17 for teaching annotation). Encourage them to look for the purpose of each paragraph.

Step 4: After steps 2 and 3 are completed for the whole document, group students in threes to discuss what they marked during annotation. Move throughout the room, facilitating discussions. Point out the document's capitalized words to get students talking about why certain words were capitalized.

Step 5: Challenge the groups to re-write the Declaration of Independence, paragraph by paragraph, in their own language as if it were a breakup letter. They should use their annotation about the purpose of each paragraph to structure their breakup letter. Once each group is finished, the teacher can work through pieces of the Declaration of Independence bit by bit, asking student groups to share phrases from of their breakup letter that correspond and combining the best of each into one shared breakup letter written by the whole class.

Step 6: Use a Socratic circle or fishbowl activity (details for both to follow) to discuss what is the most important word in the whole Declaration of Independence. Have them begin by identifying the most important paragraphs, then the most important phrases in those paragraphs, and finally picking out individual important words until the group can agree on the one most powerful word in the document. Forced agreement gets students questioning and challenging each other until they reach a unanimous conclusion. Students in the outer circle of the Socratic circle or "fishbowl" are questioning rather than critiquing, which leads to more productive peer feedback.

Step 7: Independently, students can use the nine-diamond ranking chart (details to follow) to write a summary of the Declaration of Independence.

See the next few pages for detailed explanations of the underlined strategies included in the multi-step lesson on the previous page.

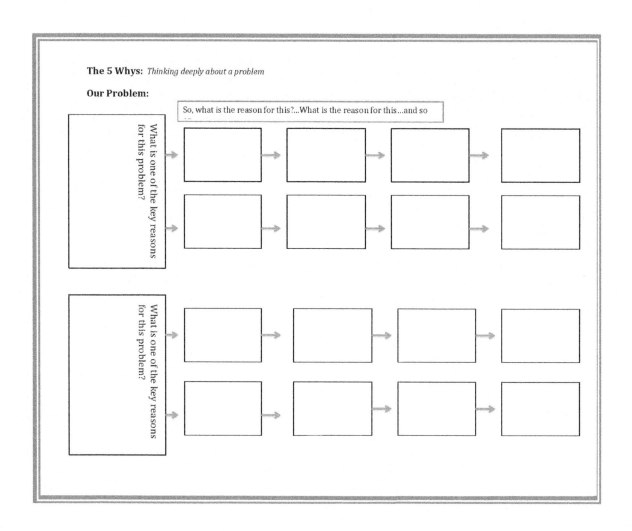

Socratic Circle

How to Use

Students form inner and outer circles. The inner circle engages in discussion about the text. The outer circle observes the inner circle and takes notes on topics they would like to discuss. Members of the outer circle can use an observation checklist or a prepared note-taking form with topics listed on it to monitor the participants in the inner circle. These tools will provide structure for listening and give the outside members specific details to discuss later in the seminar. The outer circle then shares their observations and questions the inner circle with guidance from the teacher/facilitator. Student must use questions as opposed to making judgments. The teacher may also sit in the circle, but at the same height as the students.

When to Use

- When you are trying to go in depth on a topic and have students build on each other's observations
- When you want students to see multiple sides of an issue
- When you want to introduce a new topic, Socratic circle functions as a verbal pre-assessment
- After reading text, watching a video clip, or just to generate discussion on a topic

Fishbowl

This is a variation of the Socratic circle that works especially well for younger students who may need help generating thoughtful questions, or for classes at any age that need more equitable participation. This technique prompts all students to explain their reasoning, reflect on their learning, summarize main ideas or apply a concept to a new context.

How to Use

Before class, print a list of numerous question stems (see list below), cut them out individually, fold them in half, and put them inside a fishbowl. Place the bowl on a desk or table during class. Write a topic or theme on the board for students to think about, and instruct each student to draw one question stem from the bowl. Give them three minutes to come up with a few good questions that complete their question stem and relate to the topic on the board. Next, have students stand in an inner and outer circle, facing each other like they would in speed dating. Then conduct a "3-minute face-off," with each pair of facing students asking their questions and responding to them before a timer signals it is time for the inner circle to rotate to the next person. Repeat the process a few times, as time allows.

When to Use

- As a warm-up activity to discuss a previous lesson or homework assignment, or a review at the end of a lesson or unit
- After listening to or reading about a complex concept, to help students process what they have just heard or read
- During class discussions that need a little help to get "off the ground"
- As a clarification tool for a complex problem or new guiding question posed by the teacher

Fishbowl Questions

Consider the following higher-order question stems, and add to your fishbowl those that work for your topic:

1. Can you show/tell me another way to_____?
2. If you knew the answer to _____, what would you say?
3. How is _____ similar to/different from _____?
4. What are the characteristics of _____?
5. In what other way might we show/illustrate _____?
6. What is the big idea/key concept that connects _____ & _____?
7. How does _____ relate to _____?
8. What ideas/details can you add to _____?
9. What is wrong with _____?
10. How can you "punch a hole" in the logic of_____?
11. What might you do differently if you conducted/designed _____?
12. What conclusions might be drawn from _____?
13. What question was _____ trying to answer? What problem was _____ trying to solve?
14. What do people assume about _____?
15. What might happen differently if _____?
16. What criteria might you use to judge / evaluate_____?
17. What evidence supports _____?
18. How can we prove _____?
19. How could we disprove _____?
20. How might this be viewed from the perspective of _____?
21. How would someone 20 years older/younger view _____?
22. How would someone from _____ culture see _____ differently?
23. What alternatives to _____should be considered?
24. What approach strategy could you use to _____?
25. How else could you say _____?
26. What makes _____popular?
27. What does _____remind you of?
28. Who do you know who thinks the same way as _____ (character/person/group)?
29. If you could be any of the characters/people we've studied, whom would you choose to be? Why?
30. Were there any parts of this work that were confusing to you? Why do you think some parts were confusing?
31. If you could have made any one of these discoveries, which one would you want ownership of? Why?
32. What do you feel is the most important word, phrase, or passage in this reading? Why?

Nine-Diamond Ranking Chart

Purpose: To prioritize a list of nine statements, story details, or pictures in order of importance.

Procedure: Write items to be ordered on a separate piece of paper for reference (if you are filling in the chart), or individually on index cards (if you are creating the chart on a board). Place the most important item at the top and the least important at the bottom. Place the two next most important below the top and the two next least important above the very bottom, with the three remaining in the middle being neither important nor unimportant. The nine elements will form a diamond, with the most important at the top.

For the Declaration of Independence lesson above, students would have a list of words or phrases that the class had deemed important during the Socratic circle activity. They would fill out the nine-diamond chart to organize the important words and phrases based on what they had concluding during the discussion.

Challenge Questions:

1. Does pressure to move through lots of material hinder you from diving into material multiple times and giving students adequate "reciprocity" time?

2. Can you find a DOK 3 or 4 lesson that has been crammed into a too-short time slot, and break it into parts, spreading it out to maximize both learning and efficiency?

Discuss your responses with other teachers.

10. GRANT AUTONOMY

Our inability to teach deep thought on command doesn't render us powerless to help develop it. To reach DOK 3 and 4, the teacher should step back into the role of facilitator, supporting the learning process while giving control to the student. We are not saying that direct instruction should be thrown to the wayside. Quite the opposite: we are saying that effective direct instruction should be chunked into brief segments, coupled with continual opportunities for students to construct meaning for themselves. Autonomy plus support empowers students.

Models, not Blueprints

In their book *A Perfect Mess*, Eric Abrahamson and David H. Freedman tell the story of architect Frank Gehry, whose acclaimed designs (including the Guggenheim Museum in Bilbao, Spain, among other wonders) rely heavily on evoking emotions from people who encounter his buildings. In 2002, Gehry designed a perfect scale model for an unconventional new building at Case Western Reserve University. The contractors admired the model, then asked Gehry's team for the blueprints. They thought it was a joke when told there were none. Gehry's team insisted that the contractors should study the model to derive the measurements they needed. Because Gehry's design relied more on emotion and impression than on accurate angles or measurements, he felt that to hand a two-dimensional drawing to the builders would undermine the delicate impression that came from the three-dimensional model. Without blueprints, the contracting teams would have to engage their own creativity throughout the building process in order to transfer the "feel" of the model to the finished product. It was much more involved work, but it turned out to be more innovative too. Contractors and architects worked together to bring the model to life, developing new framing techniques, new material treatment procedures, a new approach to surveying construction sites, and a new assembly method for metal panels. Most of the contracting teams involved in the project ultimately changed the way their businesses operated thanks to their inventions. They had been pushed into innovation because they were challenged to structure the big picture of the project themselves, rather than following a mechanized set of instructions. By giving the contractors more autonomy, the architect had achieved exactly the vision he wanted and had allowed the contractors to reach the depths of knowledge where innovation and discovery can be found (Abrahamson, 2006).

> In complex thinking tasks, the person doing the work must have ownership of the process.

Give your students models, not blueprints, when you're hoping to reach DOK 3 or 4. This is hard to do, because it means giving up some control over how the work is done. That doesn't mean giving up control over the ultimate assignment: Frank Gehry wanted the finished building to have exactly the look and feel of the model, and he didn't compromise that demand. It means, rather, that you give up some control over the creative mental process used to get there. In complex thinking tasks, the only way to achieve the desired outcome is for the person doing the work to have ownership of the process.

Give students models, not blueprints.

Autonomy, with support, sends the message that you trust your students. And trust you must. If you never put students in the driver's seat during daily discussion and problem-solving, how will they develop the resilience needed to work through difficult text and text-dependent questions when the stakes are high? Autonomy gives them a chance to develop time management skills and practice the art of collaboration, and it also motivates students (Pink, 2009). They may go about their learning in a messy, unconventional way, but doing it themselves leads them to take ownership, which is necessary for breaking through the barriers to deeper thinking.

Autonomy and Motivation

Daniel Pink argued in his 2009 bestseller, *Drive*, that many businesses operate under outdated ideas of "management," and his argument is applicable to the classroom. He says that for rule-based or routine tasks (that is, DOK 1 and 2 thinking tasks), people are motivated by what he calls "carrots and sticks," or external rewards and punishments. In education, this could be grades, gold stars, praise from teachers, or simply the feeling of knowing the "correct" answer. But for more complex or creative tasks (DOK 3 and 4), people perform better when they have more freedom to choose what to do, when and how to do it, and whom to do it with. In fact, traditional efforts to "manage" people backfire when the tasks are of this sort. They lose motivation, cheat, and have trouble thinking outside the box (Pink, 2009). To reach strategic and extended thinking, and encourage intrinsic motivation and a love of learning, autonomy is key.

Become a Facilitator

But that autonomy must be balanced with support. The task must be clear and purposeful to the student, and the challenges must be "just right" for the student: not too hard, not too easy.

Many teachers are experts at the soft skill of facilitating, asking the right questions that encourage a student to make his own meaning. Give actionable feedback. Any support you offer should be given with the idea that students can use it to take action. While you are facilitating autonomous work, keep your feedback actionable. During the DOK 3-4 process is not the time for evaluations of the produced work. Keep any praise during this time focused on the student's process or actions, rather than on the work or outcome. Keep any criticism constructive, prompting thoughtful responses by asking questions rather than pointing out mistakes (see module 19 for specifics on giving feedback). This kind of facilitating is where teaching becomes an art. It is grueling work, but take the time and energy you would normally spend "managing" your students or giving "blueprints," and use that energy instead on facilitating.

Tips for Autonomy

- **De-emphasize grades in DOK 3 and 4 work**. Grades may motivate work at DOK levels 1 and 2, but they are not productive for DOK 3 and 4. Instead, give plenty of autonomy, a clearly-explained purpose, and challenges that are well matched to students' abilities. If you're worried that students will not do the work without a grade, embed formative assessments instead (see module 12 for specific tools). For some activities you can use time as a motivator: students who are motivated by grades usually also are motivated by timed competitions.

- **Rearrange the classroom**. Avoid a traditional teacher-centered classroom seating design during DOK 3-4 lessons so your students feel free to participate and collaborate.

- Use **modeling** and **gradual release** ("I do it, we do it, you do it") as tools for autonomy (Hess, 2009). First show your students how you think through a complex problem, or think aloud when summarizing a text. Show, don't tell. Then, go through it together, helping them along. Finally, give them control to do the work on their own. See module 16 for more on modeling your thinking.

Graphic Organizer Challenge

Loosely structured frames, like charts and graphic organizers, can be a great tool for providing autonomy with support, and for an emphasis on autonomy we recommend challenging students to choose which graphic organizer works best. Whether they are reviewing vocabulary words, summarizing text, or taking notes during a class discussion, selecting the best graphic organizer for the assignment adds rigor and autonomy, and it also gets them thinking about how they think (we discuss metacognition in module 16).

How to Use

Provide students with several full-page printed graphic organizers to choose from (see the list below). During or at the end of a lesson, allow students to take notes using their organizer of choice. Afterwards, engage them in a class discussion comparing the different organizers.

When to Use

- When you want to provide some structure for a lesson while allowing the student to do the cognitive organizing
- As an equitable check for understanding that pushes all students into strategic thinking about the relationships between words, elements, or concepts
- When you want students to categorize and classify information in their own ways
- During class discussions as a way for students to organize ideas before sharing them with the class
- As a closing activity so that students can review what was learned in the lesson
- As a clarification tool for a complex problem or new guiding question posed by the teacher

14 Graphic Organizers

1. AFFINITY DIAGRAM
Purpose: To group ideas into categories or themes.
Procedure: Record the results of a brainstorm by placing an organizing theme or heading in the top boxes. Write similar concepts or items below each theme or heading.

2. CONCEPT MAP
Purpose: To define a concept by identifying its elements or attributes.
Procedure: Write the concept in the center circle. Record its attributes or elements in the outer circles

3. CONSEQUENCES CHART
Purpose: To explore options when making decisions.
Procedure: Start with a 'what if' question or problem and write it in the circle on the left. Students suggest solutions to be written in the middle circles and the possible consequences of each in the circles on the right.

4. FISHBONE DIAGRAM
Purpose: To provide a systematic way of considering a problem.
Procedure: Write the problem in the fish's 'head'. Use the 'bones' for the questions – how, when, where, why and what. *Tip: You can modify this diagram to incorporate a different Edward de Bono 'thinking hat' at the end of each stem to direct students' thinking (The deBono Group, 2016).*

5. FLOW CHART
Purpose: To represent a sequence of events.
Procedure: Write or draw events in order in each box. Other boxes can be added to show related events.

6. FUTURE LINES
Purpose: To consider two possible futures.
Procedure: List aspects of a probable future if things were to continue as they are now, and ideas about what the future could be like if particular actions were taken to shape it.

7. PNQ
Purpose: To evaluate thoughts about an issue and clarify issues for further investigation.
Procedure: Students list the "Positives" of an issue in the first column, the "Negatives" in the second column. In the third column, they list "Questions" for further investigation.

8. PLACEMAT

Purpose: To consider one's own opinions before negotiating a group response to an issue.
Procedure: Each group member has a section to write in. The square in the middle is to record the group response. Students are given an issue, topic or question to consider. They record their individual responses. They share their responses and as a group decide the response to be recorded in the middle.

9. NINE-DIAMOND RANKING CHART

Purpose: To prioritize a list of nine statements or pictures in order of importance.
Procedure: List items to be ordered on a separate piece of paper. Choose the most important and write it in the top of the diamond, then write the least important at the bottom of the diamond. Place the two next most important and two next least important near the top and bottom respectively, with the three remaining in the middle.

10. WEB MAP

Purpose: To assist in activities that involve planning, brainstorming, making notes, organizing or problem solving.
Procedure: An issue or topic is written in the center. Related ideas are linked to the central issue and other ideas are developed from these. Use lines, colors, labels and arrows to show links between ideas.

11. VENN DIAGRAM

Purpose: To compare the similarities and differences between two or more groups of people, places or issues.
Procedure: Write the items being compared in the circles. Where the circles overlap, record similarities. Record the characteristics which are different in the areas that do not overlap.

12. X-CHART

Purpose: To brainstorm ideas based on what we would see, hear, smell and feel in a given situation.
Procedure: List ideas in each section as labeled – looks like, sounds like, smells like, feels like.

13. PMI

Purpose: To evaluate thoughts about an issue and clarify questions for further investigation.
Procedure: Students list the "Pluses" (positives) of an issue in the first column and the "Minuses" (negatives) in the second column. In the third column, they list elements that cannot be classified precisely as positive or negative as "Interesting."

14. Y-CHART

Purpose: To brainstorm ideas based on what we see, hear and feel.
Procedure: List ideas in each section as labeled – looks like, sounds like, feels like.

Challenge Questions:

1. How do your directions limit student thinking? Are your instructions to students "models" or "blueprints"?

2. Do you find it unnerving to give students autonomy?

3. How do you define *actionable feedback*?

4. Do you think you ask more questions or point out more mistakes?

5. Can you think of a classroom activity you have used that might be revamped to give students more control of the process, and to allow you to spend more time facilitating and less time managing?

Discuss your responses with other teachers.

11. LEVERAGE PEER FEEDBACK

Many classrooms today give students opportunities to talk. But for that talk to lead to learning, it must be **productive talk**. Productive talk means teachers structure conversations in which students construct meaning for themselves. It includes questioning, listening to and challenging others, and making connections aloud.

Many teachers, in an effort to engage all their students and hoping for such productive conversations, encourage peer feedback. When students are instructed to give each other feedback on projects or ideas, often their first tendency is to give evaluative feedback: "This is pretty good." But more productive than evaluative feedback is directive or descriptive feedback.

<u>Directive feedback:</u> Suggesting specific actions or changes to make, or the next steps to take on a project. Directive feedback leads to the listener taking action.

Examples: "What if you combined these two sentences?" "Have you thought about adding a funny opening to your presentation?"

<u>Descriptive feedback:</u> Pointing out details about the work; Specifically pointing to gaps in understanding or aspects of the work that show the student's thought process. Descriptive feedback leads to the listener coming up with specific actions or next steps on his or her own, or explaining his or her thought process.

Examples: "I'm not sure how these two sentences are related." "I see how you've organized this presentation chronologically instead of by topic."

Leverage peer feedback by teaching students how to give feedback effectively. Just as DOK 3-4 thinking time is not the time for the teacher to evaluate the student's work, it is not the time for peers to criticize or praise it. Both descriptive and directive feedback should lead to action rather than evaluation. Teach these terms to students. Teach your students to give feedback that is actionable by asking questions and figuring out the worker's thought process rather than focusing on the work produced. See Module 18 for specific prompts and phrases to teach students how to give helpful feedback.

> Don't just enourage peer feedback. Make it productive and leverage it.

On the following pages are a few instructional strategies that teachers can use to create an environment rife with opportunities for peer feedback. Teach students how to give helpful feedback while they are engaged in these activities. Combined with the prompts in Module 18, these strategies provide an ideal environment for productive talk.

Think-Pair-Share

There are endless ways to adapt Think-Pair-Share, but here is the basic structure.

How to Use
1. Think - Pose a question or topic related to the lesson that has many possible responses. Then have students individually brainstorm five possible answers or things they know about the topic.
2. Pair - Ask students to work in pairs to share their lists and then decide on the three best answers or ideas from their two lists.
3. Share - Instruct the pair to join with another pair to choose the response that best represents the group. *List the feedback prompts (module 18) on the board and remind the groups that to choose the "best" response they will need to analyze the thought process behind each response, which will make their talk productive.*

When to Use
- At any point in the lesson to structure meaningful conversation
- Before introducing new material to tap into prior knowledge
- After watching a film clip to gauge a reaction
- After reading a short text or guiding question to begin a discussion or upcoming lesson

The Carousel

The carousel is an extended version of Think-Pair-Share. If you take out traditional seating and give autonomy, added to multiple intelligence instruction styles, think-pair-share comes alive and becomes dynamic.

How to Use

You will need a timer or clock, different colored markers, and large sheets of paper posted around the room with some distance between them. On each paper, write different question or statement that can elicit a broad range of responses. Divide your students into 4-5 teams and give each team a different colored marker. Send each group to one posted question, and instruct them as follows: "When I say go, you will have two minutes as a group to write as many intelligent points as you can on your board. When I call time, every group will take their marker and rotate to the left, just like a carousel. When you get to the next paper, before you write anything, read through what the other group(s) have written. If you disagree with something they have written, put one line through that statement and then begin to post your own thoughts." Continue rotating until all groups have responded to every question, and then facilitate a class discussion afterwards, reminding students of the feedback prompts in module 18. Students will engage in productive talk within groups as well as in a class discussion afterwards. All it takes to get great conversation going on this is a couple of lines drawn through comments of another color.

When to Use

- When your students need a lesson that gets them on their feet
- When your topic is broad and multi-faceted
- As a pre-assessment when introducing a topic
- As a review game before a summative assessment

Post-it Note Tug-of-War

How to Use

This is a collaborative whole-class activity in which the classroom wall serves as a platform for post-it notes. Divide the class into two groups, and give four or five Post-it notes to each student. Choose any two content items to be compared, posting a visual to represent each item on the wall. One group will be assigned to each content item. The challenge is for the students to post as many details or descriptive ideas to their side as possible during a timed race. As the teacher, you will be the "knot" in the tug-of-war rope, moving to the side of the wall with the most Post-its. The side with the most Post-it notes wins.

When to Use

- To compare and contrast any two big ideas, characters, historical figures, scientific theories, or statistical reasoning data
- Before encouraging students to solve a problem or make a prediction, as a way to lead students to find the root causes
- In group decision-making, to evaluate two opposing arguments

Challenge Questions:

1. Do your students know how to give each other helpful feedback?

2. During peer feedback activities, do you encourage students to try to understand the thought process of the person whose work they are looking at?

3. What steps have you taken to ensure a classroom environment in which students feel safe to give and receive peer feedback?

Discuss your responses with other teachers.

12. EMBRACE FAILURE

"The right to fail is just as important as the right to succeed: children must be encouraged to experiment and to learn from their intellectual mistakes and failures without punishment. They must be free to be children." -James Meredith, American civil rights icon and public school advocate (qtd. in Strauss, 2016)

Create Failure Opportunities

Most of us understand intuitively that failure can be an opportunity to learn, but even the most optimistic of us often see failure as a necessary evil, something that, with a positive attitude, can be redeemed into a learning opportunity. We'd prefer never to fail, but if it must happen, we'll find the lesson in it.

But recent research goes further, suggesting that failure is actually highly beneficial to the learning process and teachers should intentionally incorporate failure into their lesson designs. Neuroscientists have discovered that when you make a mistake, your brain gets a boost: nearly twice the number of neurons fire as usual, giving you a deeper understanding and making lasting connections in your brain (Rutherford, 2013). To get students thinking at DOK levels 3 and 4 and promote real learning (and, incidentally, better preparation for today's tests), we must make routine use of the benefits of failure.

Lesson design must anticipate failures that will be productive. To incorporate productive failure, the general structure of a lesson should follow this model, adapted from the principles of productive failure created by professor of psychology Manu Kapur (Education University of Hong Kong):

- Anchor tasks in prior knowledge but do not entirely rely on it.
- Assign tasks that draw on multiple ideas or texts, or provide multiple paths for students to think through them.
- Ensure that students have the ability to work on the task but not to solve it. They need to encounter obstacles that will help them identify what they don't know and what they need to find out to solve the problem. This process should rely on the students' own further reasoning (DOK 3 strategic thinking).
- Anticipate failure after a productive struggle, and build time for failure into the lesson design.
- Instruct students in the missing information, or rather ask guiding questions so they can figure out the solution.
- Allow students to complete the task on their own.
  (Schwartz, 2016)

Cultivate an Abundance Mindset

Many students operate under the assumption that success is scarce, looking at class rank and test score percentiles as measures of success. Those data measures can be important tools for schools to understand their progress, but they should not be taken to mean that any student's success in learning depends on the failure of another. Stephen Covey calls this idea the scarcity mindset. It kills learning because it puts people on the defensive and prohibits the sharing of ideas. Its opposite, the abundance mindset, tells people that there is success enough for everyone, and that we'll all get there faster if we help each other out. Students who act out this mindset are not afraid to ask questions and share their ideas, because they know people are rooting for them (Covey, 1989).

To cultivate an abundance mindset in your students, make your classroom a haven of security, where failure is simply a part of the process. Don't save your hardest questions for the test. Students learn best when they work through hard questions in daily practice. You wouldn't put a new driver on the road alone until they'd seen the hazards of driving in practice with an adult in the passenger's seat. If your students sail through their formative assessments but struggle with high-stakes summative tests, they likely need more daily practice navigating through complex thinking work, even if that means more chances of ending up in a ditch. Give them those opportunities to fail when the stakes are low. Students who fail more often ultimately succeed.

> Productive failure is at the heart of strategic thinking.

Embracing productive failure is at the heart of creating a classroom culture that promotes strategic thinking. Without the freedom to fail, students cannot focus on their thought processes because they're too worried about the outcome. They can't take ownership of their learning because then there would be no one to blame if they did not succeed. They can't collaborate effectively because their mindset of scarcity tells them that only a few can succeed. Doing right by students includes creating opportunities for failure.

De-emphasize Grades

American education has a twisted love affair with grades. Everyone seems to hate them and acknowledge that they don't accurately measure learning, yet we can't stop depending on them to determine our progress and worth. Teachers are under external pressure from school districts, principals, parents, and students who, with no other recourse for evaluating education, demand to see performance boiled down to a single letter. You can't avoid grading students, but to get them thinking deeply you must de-emphasize grades, especially during DOK 3 and 4 lessons.

Grades may seem like an important motivator because outcome-driven students will work hard for them, but when it comes to the kind of intrinsic motivation that's necessary for deep thinking, grades fall short. An obsession with grades prevents students from focusing on the thought process, and it lets high ability students off the hook for deep thinking, since they often know how to achieve a good grade without any sort of productive struggle. If you are deliberately structuring lessons that anticipate failure for learning's sake, a focus on grades will prevent students from taking ownership of the learning and entering strategic thinking.

Emphasize Learning with Thoughtful Rubrics and Formative Assessments

Convince students that learning, rather than a high grade, is the desired outcome. The way to do that is by embedding formative assessments into lessons and creating thoughtfully designed rubrics to better assess the nuanced, organic process of learning. Some schools have begun including these intangibles on their scoring rubrics, assessing students on how well they take ownership of their learning. New Tech Network, which works with public school districts to create innovative schools, calls that ownership "agency," and New Tech schools have a specific rubric to measure for it. The agency rubrics look at how readily a student practices skills, how long a student keeps practicing before asking for help, whether she seeks challenges, analyzes and overcomes her own personal mindset barriers, recovers from setbacks, and connects her schoolwork to her personal goals and experiences (New Tech Network, 2016). Measuring agency may be a somewhat flimsy science, but it communicates to students the importance of learning, and a grade that takes agency into account is one step closer to an authentic assessment of learning.

Work with teachers in your school to design more thoughtful rubrics, and embed formative assessments as a low-stakes way to monitor learning and target areas that need work. Here are a few suggestions of physical tools for embedding formative assessments, with more detailed explanations on the following pages.
- Entrance cards
- Exit cards
- Talk tickets
- Individual dry-erase boards
- Hypothetical real-world scenarios

Entrance Cards

How to Use

Stand in the doorway or just outside your classroom, and as students enter your room, hand them each an index card. You will have posted a problem or question on the board waiting on them. Say, "Good morning. Please take this card and use it to write your response to the problem on the board in as much detail as possible. It's not for a grade, so just try your best." Return entrance cards to students and encourage them to keep the cards as a study aid.

When to Use
- When you want to connect the day's learning objectives to the previous day's learning or to connect a previous theoretical lesson to a lesson on its practical application
- To informally assess understanding of a concept introduced the previous day

Exit Cards

After several months of regularly using exit cards, a local teacher we know commented, "You know, I just realized today that my students have stopped asking me, 'Is this for a grade?' I never hear that anymore!"

How to Use

A twist to the entrance card, only you are using it at the end of class. With close to 5-7 minutes left in the class, post some aspect of the day's learning to "quiz" them over. Sometimes it is effective to read the responses aloud (without divulging names) so that students hear the pertinent information one last time. The exit cards function as both a review and a quick check for understanding, and they can be kept and collected throughout the semester to be used as flashcards for review.

When to Use
- When you have a few extra minutes at the end of class
- When you need to assess understanding with low stakes
- As a clarification tool for a complex problem or new guiding question posed by the teacher
- As a closing activity so that students can review what was learned in the lesson and create a collection of cards to study from

Talk Tickets

How to Use

Create cardstock "talk tickets" to allow for equitable verbal assessments. Distribute tickets to students at the beginning of each day or week. Say, "Everyone gets two tickets per day, and you must spend them speaking in a group or one-on-one to the teacher." Students who naturally talk less are more likely to do so with a physical reminder, and students who naturally talk more or ask questions to which they already know the answers will be forced to think first and make their conversations more meaningful.

When to Use
- As an informal assessment tool during class discussions, to ensure you will hear from everyone
- With an entire class or only with particular students who need to be brought into more meaningful participation

Individual Dry Erase Boards

How to Use

Provide each student with an individual dry erase board to collect student responses during Q&A sessions, so that every student gets the chance to complete the thought process before the class moves to the next question. Instruct all students to hold up their answers rather than waiting for just one or two raised hands to answer verbally. Expect an answer from everyone so you can use it as a quick assessment.

When to Use
- As a formative check for understanding during Q& A
- During verbal quizzes, verbal cues, and whiteboard brainstorms. All students are held accountable to give a response.
- As a preparation for group discussion. All students can be held accountable to prepare an answer on their board so they have something to share with the group.
- When students need to organize information, whiteboards can be used to create graphic organizers that can be easily shared with the class.

Hypothetical Real-World Scenarios

How to Use

Distribute cards to student groups with printed scenarios (see examples below), one for each group. They will be forced to infer meaning and collaboratively justify the best course of action, skills that exemplify strategic thinking. According to John Maxwell's *Thinking for a Change*, strategic thinking is at the heart of effective planning, which involves the following steps:

1. Breaking down the issue
2. Asking *why* before *how*
3. Identifying the real issue and objectives
4. Reviewing the resources
5. Developing your plan

Instruct students to use these five steps to work through the following scenario cards and engage in strategic thinking.

- **Scenario 1A** - Imagine you are currently employed as a hazardous materials technician and are now being interviewed for a promotion. You interviewed so well that they have offered you your choice of either a SPECIALIST LEVEL POSITION or an INCIDENT COMMANDER (IC). How will the tasks, skills, and responsibilities of those 2 positions differ? List as many points as you can that you would need to consider before taking one of the two promotions. Defend your ultimate job choice. Choose wisely!

- **Scenario 1B** - Your crew responds to a report of a suspicious odor at a small plastics manufacturing company. When you arrive, you notice a tractor-trailer delivery truck parked at the loading dock, with the motor still idling. You can see only one side of the trailer. It has a red diamond-shaped placard on it that reads "FLAMMABLE," with a number 3 on the bottom. You notice the odor as soon as you roll down the window. The facility security guard reports that several people can smell something like "paint thinner" in the air. List at least 7 QUESTIONS you and your partner have to ask before responding accurately to the situation. What are your CLUES to direct your thinking?

When to Use
- To encourage collaboration and push students into DOK level 3
- To embrace failure in a low-stakes activity (Ensure that the scenario includes some unfamiliar words as well as real-world situations that students would not have encountered themselves.)

Challenge Questions:

1. Do you talk to your students about embracing mistakes, and then follow through by giving them plenty of chances to fail productively?

2. How can you model for students the process of identifying their mistakes in a way that is productive, not prohibitive, to learning?

3. Are you afraid to let your students fail because of how it might reflect on you as their teacher?

4. What is one specific tool you can adapt in your classroom to embed formative assessments and reduce the focus on grades?

5. Look at your formative and summative data. Do many of your students do much better on one than the other? What could you do to ensure that the rigor of your formative and summative assessments matches up?

Discuss your responses with other teachers.

13. FOCUS ON PROCESS, NOT OUTCOME

The change from DOK 1-2 to DOK 3-4 is significant primarily because it is a change in focus: from valuing outcomes to valuing processes. We talked in module 12 about embracing failure in our classrooms. But it's simply impossible to remove the fear of failure if daily instruction focuses on outcomes and grades rather than on the learning process itself (William, 2011). As it turns out, we will need to pay more than lip service to the idea that the process matters more than the grades. Closing the gap between DOK 2 and DOK 3 poses this challenge: we must spend significant portions of instructional time in activities that de-emphasize grades if we have any hope of deepening student thought. Embed formative assessments into the lesson, rather than grading assignments (see module 12 for tools for embedding formative assessments).

De-emphasizing grades to eliminate the fear of failure is part of this larger focus on process rather than outcome. But it is more than that. Focusing on the process means you as the teacher are more concerned with what is happening in the students' minds than with what they are producing to turn in. In daily instruction, as well as in extended projects, make it your goal to see evidence of a student's thought process, rather than to see an end product. That doesn't mean the end product will suffer. On the contrary: shoot for outcome and you only get outcome. But shoot for process and you get both.

Expect an Answer from Everyone

One small way to communicate to students that you're concerned with what's happening inside their heads rather than with the end product is to change the way you call on students during question-and-answer sessions. Often when a teacher questions a group of students, the students get the impression that what the teacher wants is an answer. They wait for one person to give an answer so the teacher can move on to the next question. But what the teacher really wants is for everyone to engage in the thinking process to find an answer. Give each student an individual dry-erase board. Instead of calling on whoever raises a hand, expect an answer from everyone. Instruct all students to write an answer on their dry erase board and hold it up. Then wait a few extra seconds until each student has something written before calling on someone. This is a minor change, but it communicates to students that your goal is for everyone to think through the question, rather than for someone to find the answer. A focus on the process fosters the mindset that success is abundant and leads to equity.

Emphasize the Process with Note-Taking

People who value their thought processes often record them by taking notes that represent how ideas are related or organized in their minds, and these notes help to form their understanding. Teach students the importance of the thought process by teaching them how to take good notes. Here are five note-taking systems you can teach your students:

1. **Outline Format**

    This is the traditional note-taking with which most students are familiar. Teachers deliver content and students take notes linearly.

2. **Interactive Notes**

    History Alive! popularized this interactive form of note-taking, where students are responsible to add to the quality of their content with ideas that reflect their natural learning styles. Students are taught a system where the right side of the page is for the content being discussed in the classroom, while the left side is reserved for their own personal connections to the content later. This forces assimilation. This is a perfect way to provide a model, not a blueprint. (*America: History of our Nation*, 2007)

3. **Cornell Notes (Two-column notes)**

    The Marzano Research Group provided evidence that this note-taking system challenges students and helps them to learn the information better. It forces them to categorize information while they absorb the content. The left column of the notes is for main ideas or categories, while the right side is for supporting details. At the bottom, students reserve an inch of space to summarize the whole page of notes. In the writing process, this is helpful because students are much less likely to plagiarize because they are already summarizing their own notes. And it teaches them that notes have a purpose: we write from our notes.

4. **Three-Column Notes**

    Due to the popularity of Cornell Notes (two-column notes), many teachers have adapted them to add a third column to fit the learning task that follows. This may be a column for making predictions, inferences, providing evidence, or synthesizing, depending on what the teacher is planning for the next step in the lesson.

5. **Sketch Notes**

    This visual note-taking process appeals to younger, information-age learners, who are most comfortable with spatially chunked content in which words and images are merged. If sketch notes are new to you, we suggest a web search to familiarize yourself, and you'll see the appeal. Allow students to personalize note-taking and make it work for them.

How Note-Taking Connects to DOK 3

An essential component of strategic thinking is understanding the structure of the content. Empower students with multiple approaches to note-taking, so they can practice choosing which style fits best with any given content.

Self-Assessment

Most of us say we care more about the learning process than the grade. But do we emphasize the learning process with our students as much as we emphasize what they are turning in?

What does note-taking usually look like in your classroom? Do you require your students to take notes? If so, do you teach them how or assume they already know? Use this space to write down the note-taking systems you have found helpful, and discuss them with other teachers.

Below you will see instructions for specific process-focused activities and tools for equitable instruction.

Four Corners

This technique stimulates student learning through movement and discussion, and it can also be used as a formative assessment. Four Corners promotes listening, verbal communication, critical thinking, and decision-making. It promotes equity by getting every student participating without giving anyone an "out."

How to Use

1. Prepare

Generate a controversial statement or a question related to your topic of study. Create four different opinions related to the statement or four possible answer choices to the question (often teachers use "Strongly Agree," "Agree," "Disagree," and "Strongly Disagree"). Post these on chart paper in four different areas of your classroom. The opinions/answers can also be shown on the overhead in multiple choice format, while each corner of the room is labeled as A, B, C, or D.

2. Present

Read the statement or problem to the class, without giving them choices. Allow time for students to independently think about an answer to the statement/question. You can ask them to write down their answer and reason for their choice. Then, provide the answer choices. Ask students to choose the option that comes closest to their original answer.

3. Commit to a Corner

Ask students to gather in the corner of the room that corresponds to their choice. In each corner, students form groups of two or three to discuss the reasons for selecting a particular choice.

4. Discuss

Allow two or three minutes of discussion. Call on students to present a group summary of their opinions. This can be done through an oral presentation or as a written statement.

When to Use
- At any point in the lesson to structure meaningful conversation
- Before introducing new material to tap into prior knowledge
- After watching a debatable film clip to gauge a reaction
- After reading a short text to begin a discussion
- In the middle of direct teaching to help students process information
- When students are in need of movement
- As a test review after a unit of study
  For a test review, place A, B, C, or D in each corner. Ask a multiple-choice question, and have students move to the answer they would choose.

Human Data Collections

How to Use

Place a strip of masking tape on the floor in your classroom that is long enough for 5 students to stand side by side on, with a comfortable space between them. You will want to tape a 1, 2, 3, 4, and 5 on the floor across the tape for students to see where they stand.

Create specific questions based on your topic of study that gauge student views. For instance, to introduce a unit on healthy living choices you might say, "Let's see a human data collection of our loves of certain foods and drinks. I'll start with chocolate. If you hate chocolate and never eat it stand in a row on number one. If you are neutral on chocolate, you would stand on 3, and if you LOVE it, you'll be standing in a row on 5." Demonstrate to students once they are standing, that we can get a good visual of our views, creating a life-size human graph.

When to Use
- When students need to stand and experience more blood flow
- As a warm-up activity to discuss a previous lesson or homework assignment
- After five to seven minutes of oral or written input, to help student process what they have just heard or read
- During class discussions as a way for students to process their opinions and ideas before sharing them with the class
- As a closing activity so that students can review what was learned in the lesson
- As a clarification tool for a complex problem or new guiding question posed by the teacher

Individual Dry Erase Boards

How to Use

Provide each student with an individual dry erase board to collect student responses during Q&A sessions, so that every student gets the chance to complete the thought process before the class moves to the next question. Instruct all students to hold up their answers rather than waiting for just one or two raised hands to answer verbally.

When to Use
- As a formative check for understanding during Q& A
- During verbal quizzes, verbal cues, and whiteboard brainstorms all students are held accountable to give a response.
- As a preparation for group discussion. All students can be held accountable to prepare an answer on their board so they have something to share with the group.
- When students need to organize information, whiteboards can be used to create graphic organizers that can be easily shared with the class

Challenge questions:

1. Do you agree with the statement that "if you focus on outcome, you only get outcome"?

2. How is equity related to having a focus on thought processes?

3. In what ways do you show your students that you care about their learning?

4. What practical activities, like note-taking, can be used to turn the focus of a lesson toward the cognitive process rather than the outcome?

Discuss your responses with other teachers.

14. TIPS FOR HIGH ABILITY STUDENTS

A classroom culture that encourages DOK 3-4 thinking is a classroom culture that engages students at every ability level. Because deep thinking gives control to the student, everyone's exploration process is a little different.

Strategic thinking is a tool for enrichment.

Struggling students can engage in strategic thinking during whole-group instruction, because DOK 3 and 4 really are not dependent on ability. However, high ability students often lose interest or finish work early because of their advanced skills. We advocate that teachers consider the structure of the learning environment and look for ways these students can increase the complexity of their work on an individual basis. Don't give advanced students more of the same when they finish early; instead, give them complex tasks and projects to complete on their own. Enrichment is not giving students more. It is not computer time, longer papers, broader canvasses to paint, lengthier discussions, or more frequent debates.

Three Approaches for Advancing Complexity

Here are three approaches for reaching high-ability students. These should be modified according to your grade level and content area.

1. Guided Instruction

Imagine a 3-ring circus approach to the classroom learning environment. Based on data from your formative and summative assessments, as well as your own observations, divide your students into 3 groups: struggling learners, proficient or advanced learners, and accelerated (high ability) learners. Group struggling students with the teacher for modeling and gradual release. Proficient and advanced students are partnered to collaborate on structured learning tasks. Accelerated learners are given more complex tasks, involving evaluation, synthesis of multiple ideas for cohesion or creation of new theories, designing an experiment, and so on.

Note: This is not tracking. Don't group students at the beginning of the year and maintain these academic groupings. Use data as an ongoing tool to group students for different instructional activities.

Guided instruction benefits all learners, but for high ability students it provides the perfect platform to explore multi-step learning tasks that would be too complex for struggling students. It is also a great opportunity for high-ability students to learn to become more self-regulated in their learning.

2. Twenty Percent Time

Structure opportunities for accelerated learners to think beyond traditional lessons. When they complete learning tasks far ahead of peers, allow them to pursue a pet project around an area of their choosing. They could have one year-long project to work on autonomously.

A common concern of teachers is that students will not use 20 percent time wisely. We recommend using learning loops to structure 20 percent time so they have accountability with peers. A learning loop would follow these steps:

- Students independently research a topic.
- Students then collaborate to discuss common performance measures and create a rubric for each other.
- Students collaborate weekly to share their research findings.
- Students engage in feedback to motivate each other toward improvement.
- Students continually evaluate peers using the rubric they created.

3. Resource Banks and Research Opportunities

Despite their high abilities, many students lack the motivation, knowledge or resourcefulness to ascertain the best opportunities for their personal growth. When high-ability students finish work at an accelerated rate, teachers can have them create individualized resource banks for opportunities and growth in the following areas:

- **Twenty-first century learning skills** - creating Excel spreadsheets, practicing interview skills, practicing presentation skills, learning to use OneDrive and OneNote, creating podcasts and multimedia presentations
- **Self-study AP opportunities** - Many students are unaware that they can earn college credit on their own time with Self-study AP. See the website listed here for more information and set up a platform for your advanced students to take advantage of this opportunity. **http://blog.prepscholar.com/self-study-ap**
- **Scholarship research and applications** - job shadowing, mentoring, youth leadership conferences, STEM opportunities, summer Writer's Guilds and internship programs.

PART 2 TAKEAWAYS

- Classroom culture must be considered when planning for DOK 3 and 4.
- Teachers should identify the DOK level of their standards for any given lesson and adjust their role accordingly, functioning as a facilitator and giving more autonomy for levels 3 and 4.
- Academic standards should be assessed through the lens of the DOK levels of the tasks they require. This allows for more purposeful, efficient, and effective lessons.
- Complexity of tasks should spiral within each lesson, and the highest DOK level of any task in a lesson should vary so that DOK 3-4 lessons are followed by DOK 1-2 lessons, and so forth.
- Teachers should plan for a multi-step approach, allotting more time for lessons that will reach DOK 3 or 4 and spreading them out to allow for mental incubation.
- A classroom culture that is conducive to DOK 3 and 4 will encourage peer feedback, embrace failure, and focus on the students' cognitive processes more than on the outcome or what they are producing.

List additional takeaways below.

3
DIVE IN: EMPOWERING OWNERSHIP

This section of the book explains how to empower students to think more deeply within the context of the right classroom culture. Here we share 5 steps for empowering learners, and for each step we provide practical tips, sample lessons, and specific skills for teaching students to think at DOK levels 3 and 4.

In This Section

15. The Key to Breaking Through: Empowering Ownership
16. Empower Ownership with Labeling
17. Empower Ownership with Systems
18. Empower Ownership with Collaborative Norms
19. Empower Ownership with Anchoring
20. Empower Ownership with Multiplicity
21. Extending into DOK 4

Where do I stand?

❏   I am skeptical that all my students can take ownership of their learning. Some will just never think deeply.

❏   I tend to want more control over the way the lesson goes, rather than giving power to the students.

❏   I have students who are eager to take ownership of their learning, and I'd like more practical advice on how to guide them.

❏   My students can take ownership of their own learning, but they struggle when working in groups.

❏   I try to keep lessons rigorous but I need help finding a balance between prior knowledge and new challenging material.

❏   I would like to give my students more opportunity for extended (DOK4) thinking across disciplines.

❏   I have success stories and lesson plans that have helped my students reach DOK 3 and 4, and I will share them with other teachers.

Discuss your responses with other teachers.

---

15. THE KEY TO BREAKING THROUGH: EMPOWERING OWNERSHIP

In the blue holes of the Bahamas, only skilled and experienced divers break through the toxic level into the deep. Each cave diver must swim on his own strength through the poisonous hydrogen sulfide solution in order to reach the oxygen-free waters where discovery awaits. In the same way, students must take ownership of their own thought processes to reach strategic thinking. In DOK 3-4 lessons, then, our job as teachers becomes empowering students to own their thought processes. We are like dive instructors: we can give them tools and skills, teach them how to collaborate well, and guide them along, but we cannot do the thinking for them.

The Three Powers

The Alliance of Community Trainers (ACT) categorizes power into three types: *Power Over* is the negative exertion of force on others. *Power Within* is having the tools and ability to do things yourself. And *Power With* is having the common ground and connection with others to do things together. (ACT, 2016) Everyone seeks some form of power, and if it's not found *within* the self or *with* others, it manifests in a struggle for *power over* people or situations.

In the context of academic learning, students who do not feel they have *power within* themselves to learn and grow, or *power with* other members of a community of learners, often seek *power over* the situation in undesirable ways. This *power over* manifests itself in a withdrawal from learning or a fight against it. Disinterest or hostility toward schoolwork may be a student's only recourse for gaining power over the learning material. If your students are reluctant learners, they are reaching for power over the situation, because, for whatever reason, they haven't been given the power to work through it. Strive to give all students the other two forms of power: power within and power with. Moments of self-efficacy have long been considered important to learning, but often when students behave disruptively teachers feel they must take away the opportunity for those moments in the interest of classroom management. We argue that reluctant learners need to be given more power, not less. Since DOK 3 and 4 cannot be "taught" the same way 1 and 2 can, teachers must, to some extent, give up their own power over their students' learning to encourage deeper thought. We do not mean to be glib about the difficulties of engaging reluctant learners. Each student's struggles are different, and many bring with them emotional and physical hardships from home. But we do believe that a great majority of disinterested students will benefit from greater autonomy and the teaching of specific skills for engaging with their classmates in a way that empowers them to take ownership of their learning. Part 3 of this book is intended as a tool to help make that happen.

Freedom within a Frame

We've talked a lot about the need for autonomy, but in Part 3 we want to emphasize the sturdy frame that will give student autonomy its support. That is, the rigid framework of habits that you teach your students, such as note-taking, mind-mapping, and following established norms that make collaboration go smoothly. In a best-selling book on French parenting, Pamela Druckerman talks about the ubiquitous concept of *le cadre*, the frame. It means providing clear, unwavering boundaries on the important things and then giving children freedom within that frame to find their own way (Druckerman, 2014). Many parents throughout history have operated under this common-sense model; it's not a uniquely French idea, but what strikes us about its use in French parenting is that it has a name, *le cadre*, and everyone seems to know it. As a result, children pick up on the fact that their parents' balance of structure and freedom is purposeful. They grow up and talk about *le cadre* to their own kids.

Perhaps your teaching style already balances autonomy with structured support. If so, we suggest it may benefit you to make your support structure perfectly clear to your students. Talk to them about what Keith E. Stanovich calls *mindware*, the "rules, knowledge, procedures, and strategies that a person can retrieve from memory in order to aid decision making and problem solving" (Stanovich, 2009). Give them a language to discuss thought processes. Give them a method for picking out important information. Teach prompts and norms so that everyone knows the way to make productive conversations happen. These kinds of structures provide a rigid frame within which students can take responsibility for their own learning, and intimate familiarity with mindware allows students to use these structures independently for years to come.

> Give students a language to discuss their thought processes.

Reflective, Focused, and Shared Thinking

Part 2 of this book sought to give you tools for breaking through *barriers of classroom culture* that keep students from owning their learning. Part 3 will seek to help you overcome *barriers of skill and practice* to that end as well. Each of the next five modules explores practical ways to empower students: using labeling, systems, collaborative norms, anchoring, and multiplicity.

As we have shared, our approach to this breakthrough involves the following process, which we will now discuss in detail over the remainder of Part 3:

1. Students engage in **reflective thinking**, empowered by metacognitive skills to understand their own minds.
2. Students engage in **focused thinking**, empowered by skilled systems for organizing their thoughts.
3. Students engage in **shared thinking**, collaborating effectively because of the reflection and focus they have done, and empowered by learned collaborative norms. The teacher facilitates equitable productive talk.
4. Students repeat the above reflective and focused thinking individually, this time evaluating information through the new lenses gained in collaboration or through the reading of multiple related texts or perspectives. The result is **strategic thinking**.

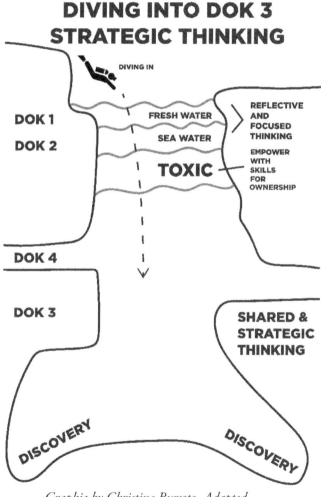

Graphic by Christine Bursoto. Adapted from images at BahamasCaves.com

Challenge Questions:

1. Do you discuss with students the various structures and strategies—*mindware*—they use to solve problems?

2. Do you think it's worth precious instructional time to talk about how we think and to put systems in place that help students understand and describe their thinking?

3. What are some systems or frames that you are already using to maintain order in your classroom? How might you create similar systems to help structure students' thinking and collaboration?

4. Do you have some students who take ownership of their learning? If so, do they seem to be cognizant of their own mental systems and strategies?

Discuss your responses with other teachers.

16. EMPOWER OWNERSHIP WITH LABELING

We've mentioned that our favorite way to push a group of students into strategic thinking is through collaboration, or shared thinking. But for shared thinking to work, each participator must bring something to contribute. So besides teaching how to collaborate well, we must teach students the skills they need to organize their thoughts prior to collaborating. Teach students to reflect and focus, giving them tools for understanding their own thought processes and organizing their ideas. Then, guide them into shared thinking as a group, and they will be better able to collaborate and break through to strategic thinking.

Encourage Metacognition

Since you will likely be spiraling complexity throughout your DOK 3-4 lessons, students will be engaged in multiple thought processes, which they need to be able to identify. Metacognition—that is, thinking about thinking—is an important part of getting to DOK 3 and 4, because it allows students to zoom out and see themselves and others from a distance, where they can think critically and evaluate multiple perspectives. The distancing effect of metacognition lets students rearrange their ideas and see how things connect. This is reflective thinking. But monitoring your own thoughts is a daunting process if you've never really thought about how your mind works. Here are two ways to encourage metacognition:

1. Model metacognition. As you demonstrate skills to your students, model your thinking aloud. Focus on the complexity of your thought process, walking through the mental steps toward understanding. "Before I can *critique* this argument, I'm going to *assess* the evidence presented. Then I'll be able to *draw a conclusion.*"
2. Give students a common language that will allow them to discuss what's going on in their minds. Teach them to label their thinking and that of their classmates. You want them to be able to say, "I disagree with you because I'm looking at the problem this way, and you seem to be looking at it that way." Encourage students to describe their mental tasks—comparing, finding evidence, making predictions—in order to turn those tasks into habits for deep thinking (mindware). This is where the verbs from the familiar DOK Word Wheel come in handy. Words like "synthesize," "analyze," "hypothesize," and so forth can become a vocabulary for students to talk about what their brains are doing.

Metacognition as a Formative Assessment

When we ask students to label their thinking, their responses tell us whether or not they are thinking strategically. If a lesson is designed to get students analyzing arguments, but the thought process they describe is not analysis, then we know the lesson design needs work. In Part 1 we mentioned that sometimes a misunderstanding of DOK leads teachers to simply change the verbs in their instruction. If all we've done is change the verb, students will not correctly identify that verb when they describe their cognitive processes. Metacognition ensures that we are designing lessons that actually get at the thinking task. Their ability to accurately label their thinking verifies to us as instructors that our lesson designs are actually translating into rigorous thought. If we have gotten them to strategic thinking, they'll be able to tell us.

Metacognition is for Everyone

Metacognitive skills are only slightly correlated to IQ, but not strongly (Stanovich, 2009). Instead, they depend on practice. There is no need to reserve this kind of thinking for advanced classes or top students. All students benefit from cognitive labeling, an important first step into strategic thinking. Here is where the DOK Word Wheel could actually be useful. Introduce the verbs on it to your students as a vocabulary lesson wrapped up in an explanation about metacognition. Have students create an anchor chart and post the verbs where your students can see them. Use them when you model your thinking, and establish an expectation that students should use them too. Explain to students that many of these verbs could be used to describe thinking tasks at multiple levels, and challenge them to think of various ways to use them. You could even make it a fun part of your classroom culture simply by ringing a "metacognition bell" whenever someone identifies a thinking process using words from the anchor chart.

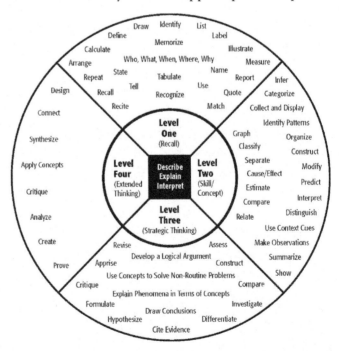

Mind Mapping

Mind maps, or concept maps, are visual representations students create to connect ideas, concepts, and terms. Students can use them to organize information they already know and to incorporate new learning with prior knowledge. Mind maps help you see how students understand content.

How to Use

1. Brainstorm
Have students brainstorm main ideas and terms related to an assigned topic.

2. Organize
Organize these ideas from general to specific. Cluster ideas or terms that are similar to one another.

3. Map
Students should write the terms in the appropriate cells of the concept map. Arrange and add cells as needed.

4. Connect
Draw arrows or lines to connect the cells that contain words that are related. Words or phrases can be connected with thicker lines to show deeper relationships.

When to Use
- With any grade level and for all content areas
- During the guided practice section of a lesson so students can synthesize information you have just covered
- As a closing activity so that students can review what was learned in the lesson
- Before a unit to access prior knowledge
- As an assessment tool or to check for understanding

Trial by Jury

How to Use

Divide students into small groups, called "juries." Read and post the following on the board:

An attorney in England, Sally Clark, was on trial for murdering her two infants, who she claimed died of Sudden Infant Death Syndrome. The pediatrician who testified to the jury included in his testimony a probability statement that made the Jury doubt it could have been SIDS. He explained that by squaring the probability of a single SIDS death, he had calculated that the odds against two children in the same family both dying of SIDS was 73 million to 1. The mother must have been lying. Sally Clark was convicted of murder and sent to prison.

But in 2003, Sally Clark's conviction was overturned and she was released from prison. Why?

1. Model metacognition to your students: "I want to start guessing answers, but first I need to step back and separate each piece of information." List the information systematically as a group.
2. Allow the "juries" to discuss the case. Encourage students to examine the logic of the pediatrician. What was his thought process?
3. Give students more information: "The pediatrician's formula for calculating probability was the correct formula for calculating the likelihood of two independent SIDS deaths in the same family." Challenge the groups to pick out the most important word in that sentence. (It is *independent*.)
4. Challenge students to find the error in the pediatrician's thought process, now that they have identified the importance of the deaths' being *independent*.
5. Give the "juries" time to discuss the case in their groups and come to a consensus. At the end of the allotted time, ask each group for their verdict: why was the pediatrician incorrect?
6. The correct "verdict" is as follows: *The pediatrician's error was in assuming the two infant deaths were independent, that no other causal factors could have affected the odds of two SIDS deaths in one family. His calculations were correct, but neither he, nor the judge, nor the jury, had taken into account the genetic and environmental factors that the babies both shared, any of which might have increased the likelihood of SIDS. (Source of story: What Intelligence Tests Miss by Keith E. Stanovich, 2009.)*
7. After the activity, challenge students to label the thought processes of the pediatrician and to label the thought processes they engaged in during the activity.

When To Use:
- When you want students to think in a non-linear way
- To encourage collaboration and forced agreement
- To encourage metacognition

In addition to reflecting on and labeling their thought processes, students can improve metacognition with graphic organizers like the 14 types listed in module 10. Over the next few pages you'll also find a table that gives practical challenges for different types of thinking across various subjects.

Label Your Thinking
Activities to encourage metacognition

Analytical Thinking demands that students analyze, evaluate, and explain information. The process of analysis is breaking down something complex so that its parts can be studied and relationships between the parts can be observed, explained, and evaluated. In the Depth of Knowledge model, our focus is on the cognitive task associated with these verbs. Essential Question: What does analytical thinking look like in your classroom?

Practical Thinking requires students to transfer and apply concepts and ideas to real-world and hypothetical real-world scenarios. In the Depth of Knowledge model, our focus is on the cognitive task associated with these verbs. Essential Question: What does practical thinking look like in your classroom?

Creative Thinking encourages students to create, imagine, synthesize and design, bringing together different perspectives, ideas, or theories to make something new. In the Depth of Knowledge model, our focus is on the cognitive task associated with these verbs. Essential Question: What does creative thinking look like in your classroom?

Research-Based Thinking requires students to autonomously explore and use a variety of strategies to retrieve information. Students must organize, closely examine relationships between concepts and synthesize ideas to create original thinking. In the Depth of Knowledge model, our focus is on the cognitive task associated with these verbs. Essential Question: What does research-based thinking look like in your classroom?

On the following pages there are a few practical suggestions of ways to incorporate these four different types of thinking across various content areas. Our suggestions will get you started. We challenge you to list additional activities you could use in your classroom.

Label Your Thinking
Language Arts

Analytical

- Compare and Contrast personality traits of two characters, themes developed in multiple texts, or text structures used to develop a plot or theme.
- Evaluate the effectiveness of the author's text; did the author achieve his purpose? Was the text structured effectively to accomplish the purpose?

Practical

- After learning various text structures and evaluating in reading and writing, apply the text structures as you write for a school newspaper, magazine, or TV show.
- Analyze, plan, and conduct Socratic circles and debates over real life scenarios/issues using textual evidence from multiple resources to justify your position.

Creative

- Imagine a character's appearance or the elements of a setting.
- Persuasive Writing - Students are fed up with the cafeteria food and have decided to do something about it. First, they research the requirements for a healthy lunch. Next, they design a menu. Finally, they create a shopping list and develop a persuasive essay or digital project.

Research-based

- Read multiple versions of Cinderella, identifying a character trait that is apparent in each version. Justify and support the trait with textual evidence from multiple versions.
- Figure out which graphic organizer to use based on the thinking required for a task, without the guidance of a teacher. Compare and contrast using a T-chart, Venn diagram, or a Double Bubble. Then explain, using textual evidence, how the author developed the same character in two different versions of the story.

Label Your Thinking
Math

Analytical
- Evaluate different methods for solving word problems and explain the method chosen.
- Pick out problems that have been solved incorrectly, identify the mistakes, then correct, and explain how and why.

Practical
- Apply math skills to the stock market, following the gains, losses, and overall profit of a company over a semester.
- Recreate a picture on a smaller scale using proportions and ratios.

Creative
- Create a dog kennel that fits a specific dog's needs and a specific budget.
- Create a stock market portfolio.

Research-Based
- Use a specific strategy to solve a math problem, without the guidance of a teacher.
- Use a KISS Box for breaking down word problems, Flip and Dip and Rocket Ship for fractions, etc. After using the strategy, then the students explain their thought process in solving the problems in written form.

Label Your Thinking
Science

Analytical
- Analyze data from an experiment and make judgments and justify with data.
- Evaluate an experiment or a theory, identify effective and ineffective steps, and explain how the results would be different if altered.

Practical
- Research an environmental issue, an animal habitat, or a problem of some sort, identify the positive factors and negative factors that are causing the problem, then develop a plan/solution that will help solve the problem.

Creative
- Design, plan, and create a habitat that would be effective for a specific animal's needs.
- Design, plan, create, and evaluate a roller coaster that applies kinetic and potential energy concepts.

Research-Based
- Analyze data and make predictions or identify trends, then explain and justify using the data.
- Argue for or against a scientific issue (genetic testing, cloning, testing on animals, etc.) using textual evidence, data, and statistics from multiple resources.

Label Your Thinking
Social Studies

Analytical

- Analyze various wars and battles and the impact the wars had on the country. Argue whether a war or battle had a positive or negative impact on the country and justify with evidence.

Practical

- After researching various battles and types of leadership, analyze a current problem in today's society, government, economy, etc. and develop a strategic plan that would help resolve the problem. Justify the solution with evidence from the research and similar previous issues to explain why your solution would be effective.

Creative

- Create a new law based on a current social issue. Then go through the "process" of getting a law passed within your classroom or grade.
- Challenge students to rewrite the rules of the game Monopoly based on life during the Gilded Age (or other time period), using evidence to support each rule.

Research-Based

- Argue for or against a law, supporting and justifying using textual evidence, data, and statistics from multiple resources.
- Annotate a social studies text, using Cornell note taking strategy to organize main ideas, then write a summary.

Label Your Thinking
Electives

Analytical

- Evaluate the effectiveness of an artist's work. Did the artist achieve his/her purpose? What was the theme or message the artist projected in the piece?
- Observe a painting and identify one element of the painting that could be removed that would not alter the artist's intent (purpose).

Practical

- Analyze and evaluate a social issue, then develop a research-based brochure, public announcement, or digital project as a solution.

Creative

- Create an exercise plan that would be appropriate for yourself (student) making sure you have a warm up, an activity that hits your "target" heart rate, and a cool down.
- Create a new game that meets specific criteria given by teacher based on skills/concepts taught.
- Design and create an autobiographical presentation using song lyrics to represent the student's life.

Research-Based

- Design and create a piece of art using specific strategies learned to reflect mood, tone, theme, etc. Explain and justify how and why the strategies impacted the piece of art.

Challenge Questions:

1. Have you ever thought about the value of metacognition?

2. What does metacognition have to do with strategic thinking?

3. How often do you model your thinking aloud for your students?

4. Can you think of practical ways your students could label their thinking?

Discuss your responses with other teachers.

17: EMPOWER OWNERSHIP WITH SYSTEMS

Putting useful skill systems in place in your classroom is a way of creating "mindware" for your students. Teach them methodical ways to take and arrange notes, to approach reading a text, and to annotate. There isn't one right way to do any of these things, but pick one and teach it to your students, because having a process for approaching various learning tasks will become a habit they can take with them and make their own over many years.

Systems allow students to engage in focused thinking. It's true that people develop their own systems for organizing ideas naturally over time, as their brains learn better executive functioning skills. But for many students that process does not happen reliably on its own until young adulthood. In the meantime, it is helpful to guide the students into organizational systems that work for them now, so that when they move into collaboration they have something to offer the group. Keeping in mind that our brains organize information much more organically than we can often explain, keep systems loose. Think of them as a tool, designed to serve the student, and if the student finds a way to adapt a system so that it works for him, let him.

Common Core Connection

Read the Common Core State Standard below. Students are expected to share information with classmates in a way that everyone can follow. The challenge for many students is not the sharing, but the preparing. It's a big job to organize organically-connected, half-developed thoughts and explain them to others. Establish mindware systems to help students practice it.

CCSS.ELA-LITERACY.SL.9-10.4
Present information, findings, and supporting evidence clearly, concisely, and logically such that listeners can follow the line of reasoning and the organization, development, substance, and style are appropriate to purpose, audience, and task (CCSSI, 2016).

Systems enable moments of self-efficacy because they give students the tools to solve problems and think on their own. Below you will find several examples of systems to adapt for your classroom, including systems for making a habit of note-taking, annotation, summarization, and inference.

Note-taking Systems

One of the most useful and underdeveloped skills for students is how to take effective notes. Teach students a basic structure for note-taking, and if you ever make notes on the board for them, try to use that same structure. Point out the location on the page of main ideas and the way you emphasize vocabulary words. For a more detailed list of note-taking systems, review the five note-taking systems we included in module 13.

Annotation Systems

Don't simply tell students to "read and annotate" text without giving them a process for doing so. Explain what types of things they might look for and annotate. Create a key, like the one shown below, to symbols they should practice using during annotation.

ANNOTATION:
Every Time We Read

? = Ask a question, something that puzzles you
  "The text mentions a DNA study. What does DNA stand for?"

!!! = Note an interesting or very important phrase or paragraph
  "I didn't realize that tapeworms can grow to 23 meters!"

C = connection to another text or piece of evidence
  "The Ebola virus is like the AIDS virus we read about yesterday because…"

*= Access prior knowledge; I already knew that!
  "I knew that photosynthesis requires water."

X = Challenge your own thinking with new information
  "I had no idea that Nobel invented dynamite."

Box it/Circle it = Words that you don't know, are repeated, or you just like
  "I've read the word ignominious and have no idea what that means—I can barely pronounce it!"

Summarization Systems

Table-talk Twitter

How to Use

Seat students in groups of four or five, each gathered around a table with a sheet of butcher paper in the center. Have one student write the session's assigned topic at the top of their paper. For instance, in a high school ELA classroom studying patterns in fictional works, you might have students write, "Characters developing by facing a trial/obstacle." Tell students, "Think Twitter. When I say 'go,' you will have six minutes to silently 'tweet' to one another, writing short, 140-character examples that fit the topic, or even tweeting from the perspective of a specific character. Respond to each other's tweets like you would on Twitter, tweeting your support or challenging an idea. You may use hashtags throughout. We can collect the hashtags at the end. Remember, no actual talking, only writing." Monitor the game closely so that you can have an effective follow-up discussion that connects several of the examples they chose to use.

When to Use
- As a refreshing change after a louder activity
- At the beginning of a lesson to pre-assess understanding
- At the end of a lecture as a way to get students summarizing the content in their own words
- As a replacement for many rote formative checks for understanding
- To cater to multiple intelligences, including intra- and interpersonal, verbal, logical, and spatial.

Summarization Systems (cont.)

GIST Summarization System

How to Use

GIST stands for Generating Interactions between Schemata and Text. In Cornell Notes (see module 13), a GIST is the summary you would write at the bottom of each page of notes, allowing you to think about the overall message.

<u>For a more guided summary:</u> After reading text, have students identify the "5 W's and an H" of journalism: Who, What, When, Where, Why, and How. Then instruct them to write the "gist" in a specified number of words, such as a 20-word GIST.

<u>For a more independent summary:</u> After a lesson, instruct students to write a 20-word summary at the bottom of their Cornell Notes that they took during the lesson. Then have students share and compare their GISTs using one of several possible methods:

    Turn & talk
    Individual dry-erase boards
    Entrance cards
    Exit cards

When to Use

- As a formative assessment of understanding essential information vs. nonessential information
- As a tool to explain the difference between paraphrasing and summarizing: the GIST should actually look like a distilled version (about 10%) of the written notes or text, while the paraphrase uses the student's own language.
- As a "chunking" tool during lectures, to allow students to stop and digest material before moving on

Inference systems

Evidence/ Interpretation Chart

How to Use

During a reading assignment, have students make a T-chart with "Facts" on the top left side and "Interpretation" on the top right. Have students fold it lengthwise so that they are only looking at the *facts* column. Instruct students to write 5-6 facts they learn as they read. Then have them turn to an elbow partner, unfold the paper, and work together to interpret the facts, returning to the text together for context clues. Encourage students to draw conclusions and make inferences that are not explicit in the text. Call on different partner teams to share their facts and how they interpreted them.

When to Use

- When students are reading complex text. *You can also use this after students have been taking notes, and have them use their notes as the text from which to gather facts.*
- When you want students to think strategically
- When the text you are reading contains many critical points that students will need as a foundation for future learning.
- As a structure to guide collaborative work
- As a check for understanding

Inference systems (cont.)

What's Going On In This Picture?

Making inferences is an important strategic thinking skill for success in the real world. But for reluctant learners or students who read far below grade level, learning to make inferences from text can be overwhelming. Don't wait until they have mastered reading to bring them into strategic thinking. Use visuals to give all students practice at making inferences and draw reluctant learners into collaboration. Thinking critically about photographs is a good exercise for students at all levels to practice the common language of labeling their thought processes, citing evidence, drawing conclusions, and justifying a response. These developed cognitive skills transfer easily to the context of reading when the student is ready.

How to Use

Produce an interesting photograph for students to examine. Ask probing questions to facilitate a discussion in which students find evidence, justify their reasoning, and separate a central idea from supporting details. Suggested photo sources: *National Geographic* magazine, *Time* Magazine, The *New York Times* Learning Network

Ask, "What is happening in this photo?"
Specifically, challenge students to engage in reflective and focused thinking with the prompt, "Take a few minutes to quietly, closely examine this image. Write what you think is going on in the photo, where it was taken, and the mood at the time. Provide three specific pieces of evidence to support your conclusions." Give students time to write. Have a student read their prediction and explain their supporting evidence. Then, ask for a student to speak out who drew an entirely different conclusion. Be sure to have every student discuss their reasoning with evidence. Also, be sure to consistently use the words *justify*, *best*, and *infer* when asking students to think deeper about what they are seeing. It is very interesting to observe how students will refine their thinking together, with minimal input from the teacher. Facilitate further with prompts based on text, tables, and other images to create self-efficacy:

- What do you notice going on in this chapter? In this diagram? Or in this political cartoon?
- What details do you see that make you say that? What evidence supports your observations?
- What more can you find in the text?

What's Going On In This Picture, cont.

Students are much less likely to be intimidated with a visual than they are with a text. Therefore, this step can be a foundation for showing what quality productive talk looks like in the classroom. The transfer of skills from talking to writing will develop.

Jennifer Bradley, a science teacher at Bentonville High School in Arkansas, told us how the practice of finding details to defend their interpretations of each photo improved students' academic skills in general, and their science skills in particular: "After practicing with "What's Going On in This Picture?" weekly, I started to see my students get much better at using evidence in their writing. For example, in their lab reports, they started to be much more detailed and to explain the context clues that led them to a conclusion."

Challenge questions:

1. If someone were to ask your students what kinds of systems or methods they use for taking notes, annotating, summarizing, and making inferences, would they be able to answer?

2. Do you have step-by-step systems posted where they are clearly visible to students? Student-created anchor charts are a great way to accomplish this.

3. Do you allow students to adapt systems to make them their own?

Discuss your responses with other teachers.

18. EMPOWER OWNERSHIP
WITH COLLABORATIVE NORMS

No one mind is as powerful alone as it is in collaboration with others. One of the most effective ways to break through the toxic layer that separates DOK 1-2 from DOK 3-4 is through shared thinking. Collaboration, when it is effective, deepens every participant's thinking. When we work alongside others, we hear their diverse thought processes and new ideas that help shape and challenge our own. This leads all involved into the comparing, evaluating, and connecting that constitutes strategic thinking.

But effective group work is a learned skill that does not come naturally to most people. Even adults are often uncomfortable with critiquing each other's work, and we hesitate to share our ideas. Let's not just hope students will pick up on implied norms that make collaboration beneficial to them. Learning how to work with others is a skill too important to leave to chance. So to reach strategic thinking, we emphasize teaching norms that will make collaboration worthwhile and effective.

Common Core Connection

Closing In on Forgotten Standards *(CCSSI, 2016)*

Read the following oft-overlooked Common Core State Standards. Students are expected to be active and competent collaborators. Lead them into creating norms for working together effectively.

CCSS.ELA-LITERACY.SL.9-10.1.A Come to discussions prepared, having read and researched material under study; explicitly draw on that preparation by referring to evidence from texts and other research on the topic or issue to stimulate a thoughtful, well-reasoned exchange of ideas.

CCSS.ELA-LITERACY.SL.9-10.1.B Work with peers to set rules for collegial discussions and decision-making (e.g., informal consensus, taking votes on key issues, presentation of alternate views), clear goals and deadlines, and individual roles as needed.

CCSS.ELA-LITERACY.SL.9-10.1.C Propel conversations by posing and responding to questions that relate the current discussion to broader themes or larger ideas; actively incorporate others into the discussion; and clarify, verify, or challenge ideas and conclusions.

CCSS.ELA-LITERACY.SL.9-10.1.D Respond thoughtfully to diverse perspectives, summarize points of agreement and disagreement, and, when warranted, qualify or justify their own views and understanding and make new connections in light of the evidence and reasoning presented.

Seven Collaborative Norms

The U.S. Department of State names seven norms for collaboration that assist in diplomacy:

1. **Pausing** - Slowing down the back-and-forth of conversation gives listeners "wait time" for improved critical thinking and better decision making. It promotes more purposeful responses and it tells others that their comments are worth thinking about. Students may be uncomfortable with silence at first, so emphasize the importance of pausing.

2. **Paraphrasing** - Translating someone else's idea into your own words helps others see your thought process, understand the idea better, and evaluate information more accurately. Paraphrasing a classmate's contribution to the discussion is also a respectful way to show you want to understand their statement.

3. **Probing** - Asking clarifying questions in an effort to understand an idea helps the whole group to think more precisely, and it shows others that their ideas are worth the effort to understand.

4. **Putting forward ideas** - Sharing original and personal contributions is vital to collaboration. Encourage everyone to share ideas, and make an effort to build up self-confidence and a sense of security so that ideas will be put forward.

5. **Paying attention to self and others** - Understanding how others process ideas leads to better partnerships. Students should make themselves aware of differences between their and others' communication styles, personal backgrounds, and ways of thinking, so that they will be able to accept disagreements.

6. **Presuming positive presuppositions** - Assuming that other group members have good intentions, even when they disagree, is necessary for productive group work. Presuming positive presuppositions allows members to "play devil's advocate" or to debate an idea without personal enmity. Impress upon students the importance of communicating positive assumptions about others.

7. **Pursuing a balance between advocacy and inquiry** - Advocating for a position must be balanced with inquiring about the positions of others. Good collaborators do both, demonstrating a desire to learn as a part of the group, and promoting equity in discussions.

(Overseas Schools Advisory Council, 2004)

The Nuts and Bolts of Feedback

In part 2 of this book, we said that a classroom culture that allows strategic thinking should leverage peer feedback. We explained the importance of making sure students have the chance to talk productively. Now we'd like to share the nuts and bolts of putting into place a system to keep their feedback actionable and their talk productive.

Even adults have difficulty seeing feedback as it is genuinely intended. When people offer verbal feedback—most of the time—it is with the intent to help. Once students can hear feedback and think, "This person is on my team!" you have succeeded in teaching a productive feedback model to your kids.

Principles for Teaching Peer Feedback

When you're teaching how to deliver feedback, stress the following four principles adapted from the work of Grant Wiggins for Educational Leadership (Wiggins, 2012).

> ## Check this out!
> Watch as Ron Berger from EL Education guides second grade students into an understanding of how to give feedback. He tells the story of a boy named Austin, whose first attempt at drawing a butterfly needed improvement. Berger takes the students through Austin's six drafts and guides them into coming up with some very specific and actionable feedback that Austin would have received from his friends. This video is a powerful illustration of how to use multiple drafts together with productive feedback.
> Source: EL Education
> https://vimeo.com/38247060

1. Feedback must be **criterion referenced**. The word "good"—as in "Good work!"—carries little meaning unless it's attached to specifics. Teach students to point out exactly what made it good, and why they thought so. Sharing their criteria for what makes something "good" keeps them focused on specifics so their feedback will be actionable.

2. Feedback is **not advice**. Establish that the receiver of feedback is the "doer," and the giver of feedback is simply prompting the doer to refine his own work. Make the distinction that advice looks like statements, while actionable feedback more often looks like open-ended questions. Have your class create anchor charts (see module 19) listing the following examples of actionable feedback and coming up with others on their own:
   - How did you mean for your tone to come across when you wrote this?
   - Why do you think I misunderstood the flow of ideas?
   - Which words in this paragraph could you change to be more specific?
   - How do you think you could have captured my interest early in your presentation?

3. Feedback should be "**bite-sized.**" Know how much feedback to deliver at any one time. Take a cue from information-age media and keep it digestible. Deliver feedback on one or two areas to consider, so the receiver can learn from it and turn it into actions. An onslaught of "helpful suggestions" can feel like an attack, which keeps the receiver from turning them into actions. Your students may find it helpful to follow this model:

    - One to praise - a specific, criterion-focused example of the student's strengths. Students, especially beginning learners, don't always know what they did well (Wiggins, 2012).
    - One to improve - an open-ended question aimed at a specific area to improve.

4. Feedback must be **timely and continual**. Thoughtful, specific, criterion-based feedback still will not be actionable if it's not given right away, when the student is in a position to use it. And if we want students to make a habit of asking themselves specific, critical, productive questions in their own work—thinking strategically—then they need to ask these kinds of prompting questions from each other often. Create an ongoing, curriculum-embedded system of opportunities for students to give this kind of feedback.

Teach these four principles as you set up an ongoing peer feedback system with frequent opportunities for students to give and receive actionable feedback.

Wonder and Yet

Improve peer feedback by teaching students two magic words: *wonder* and *yet*. *Wonder* implies possibility and ignites the imagination. During group work, saying, "I wonder why…" invites speculation and the sharing of ideas from others. *Yet* conveys faith in a person's ability to grow. When someone says, "I don't know," teach students to add "yet." Treat these as powerful magic words in your classroom.

On the following page you will find more "magic words," prompts students can use during daily discussions.

Prompts for Peer Feedback

Provide your students with a list of prompts for productive feedback. Have your students make an anchor chart to display the prompts, along with any others they can think of, and reinforce them daily by guiding students toward them when they have feedback opportunities. Here is a list of ten prompts students can use within the four principles above:

1. "What I think I heard you say was…"
2. "Did you mean for me to think that…?"
3. "How did you expect the reader/audience to react to…?"
4. "Which words do you think carry the most meaning?"
5. "Which sentence in your writing do you think is the most … (persuasive, descriptive, informative)?"
6. "Is there another way to convey this idea?"
7. "How could you reorder the steps to make this more reader-friendly?"
8. "How can you justify this part? What were your reasons for writing this?"
9. "Which of the 5 senses did you try to use to capture my attention?"
10. "Do you want to brainstorm together to come up with…?"

Making an Offer

That tenth prompt, the offer to collaborate, is especially important. Making an offer shows respect. It communicates that the person giving the feedback is not the "doer," and that taking action is the responsibility of the feedback receiver. It makes clear to the receiver that the motive behind the feedback was to empower, not to shut down. And it shows a willingness to work together and build a trusting relationship.

Student-Teacher Norms

Model the descriptive and directive feedback you are teaching. Use the words "wonder" and "yet." And when you speak to your students, check that you're conforming to the collaborative norms of pausing, paraphrasing, probing, putting forward ideas, paying attention to self and others, presuming positive presuppositions, and pursuing a balance between advocacy and inquiry. Speak affirmatively, avoiding sending subtle negative messages with words like, "You don't remember this? I taught it yesterday!" Identify your own speech patterns and build trusting relationships to enable productive feedback. This is what it means to be a facilitator.

Strategies for Improved Collaboration

In addition to the following strategies, please refer to pages 35-36 and 54 for a problem-solving frame and a 5 Whys frame, which are both excellent for collaboration.

Six Degrees of Separation

If you discuss two ideas or characters long enough, you'll almost always find a way to connect them, because neither of those two ideas exists in a vacuum. Challenge students to find connections, either between ideas in a text or between each other's perspectives. Create a "Six Degrees of Separation" flow chart to have ready for class discussions. Instruct students to fill in the chart as a kind of note-taking strategy, keeping track of the twists and turns the conversation takes.

Talk Tickets

We shared this strategy back in Module 12 as a formative assessment tool that allows you to de-emphasize grades. It's worth repeating here because it is also a simple but powerful way to make sure everyone is giving and receiving feedback.

How to Use
Create cardstock "talk tickets" to allow for equitable verbal assessments. Distribute tickets to students at the beginning of each day or week. Say, "Everyone gets two tickets per day, and you must spend them speaking in a group or one-on-one, giving actionable feedback." Students who naturally talk less are more likely to do so with a physical reminder, and students who naturally talk more or ask questions to which they already know the answers will be forced to think first and make their conversations more meaningful.

When to Use
- As an informal assessment tool during class discussions, to ensure you will hear from everyone
- With an entire class or only with particular students who need to be brought into more meaningful participation

SWOT Analysis

How to Use

Give students a blank sheet of paper, either normal size (for individual work) or large chart paper (for collaborative work), and instruct them to draw lines to create 4 blocks. They are to label the 4 blocks, *S*, *W*, *O*, and *T*, which stand for *Strengths, Weaknesses, Opportunities,* and *Threats*. Explain that the left column then is the positive column and the right hand column is the negative column. You will need to explain that opportunities are different from strengths in that they are potential positives that could be harnessed. Opportunities require a closer look at conditions and possible changes.

When to Use
- To give a solid structure for collaboration
- To examine a topic, event, or problem (either fictional or nonfictional)
- To review session an in-depth topic
- When connecting new ideas to current themes being studied
- As a self-evaluation for the group to find ways to improve
- As a launching pad into a hypothesis generating or prediction exercise so that students have given good thought to the problem or situation before predicting

Argument Frames

Teach students the following structures for presenting their arguments during discussion:

OREO	ACE
O – Opinion	A – Argument
R – Reasons	C – Claim
E – Evidence	E - Evidence
O – Opinion (restated)	

Teach them to ask the following questions when listening to someone else's opinion.

1. What information is presented that leads to a claim?
2. What is the basic statement or claim that is the focus of the information?
3. What examples or explanations are presented to support this claim?
4. What concessions are made about the claim?

Challenge Questions:

1. When your students collaborate, does everyone participate? Why or why not?

2. What kinds of collaborative norms exist in your classroom now? Did you overtly establish them, or did they simply fall into place naturally?

3. Come up with one goal for improved collaboration in your classroom.

Discuss your responses with other teachers.

19. EMPOWER OWNERSHIP WITH ANCHORING

Secure a Guide Line

The first rule of cave diving is always to "lay line." During their initial shakedown dive, divers secure a nylon guide line to formations at the surface and sink it all the way to the bottom. They keep a hand on this line at all times to ensure they'll be able to find their way back. This process allows them to venture deep down and explore in all directions without losing their way.

Thinking minds need a similar guide line, an anchor that will give us a secure place to start and a way to keep track of our roving thoughts. Learning is not the simple accumulation of new information. It is a process of adjusting prior understanding through the lens of new information, so it follows that prior understanding is a great place to start. Most teachers appreciate the need to strike a balance between simple and challenging, but providing an anchor goes deeper than that. Don't only find that "just right" level of complexity; anchor new challenges in the prior knowledge and experiences of your students to get them started.

Use Prior Knowledge Effectively

Maybe you already make a habit of assessing your students' prior knowledge using entrance cards or pre-tests, to give you an idea of where to begin teaching a lesson. But remember that for DOK 3 and 4 thinking, it is the students, not the teacher, who direct the learning and thus need to assess their own prior knowledge. Present students with the guide line of their own prior understanding so that they may grab hold of it, take ownership, and dive in.

> Students need to assess their own prior knowledge.

Sally, the third grader from module 1, noticed that water boiling down to steam was connected to the disappearance of puddles. Her mind was exploring, but her new exploration was anchored in the level 2 understanding that there is a water cycle, and that a liquid can become a gas. That prior knowledge gave Sally a place to start. It also gave her a guide line to feel her way back again later. Maybe another day, after a sweaty game of tag on the playground, Sally will notice that her skin is gritty with salt left behind from evaporated sweat. She'll hypothesize that sweat consists of a mixture of salt and water, and she'll run this hypothesis past her anchor understanding to determine that it makes sense. None of this is likely to happen if Sally is too busy thinking about new ideas to remember what she had learned about evaporation. But if, as she wipes the salty sweat from her brow, she is reminded of her earlier discovery, she may continue exploring the science of evaporation in multiple contexts.

Anchoring is a partner to the topic of our next module, multiplicity. They work together: multiplicity is the "reach" toward new information, and anchoring is the "reciprocity" that allows you to come back to where you started and see how far you went and how the two positions are related. It is much easier to re-organize new information when you can see where it came from.

Peer interview

How to Use

Introduce an upcoming topic or theme before students begin reading the text or studying the data involved in the lesson. Give students a few minutes to write 3 interview questions about the topic. Then have them find a partner to interview, writing down the person's answers. Within a specified amount of time, allow them to interview multiple classmates. Then come back together as a group and ask them to report their findings before beginning to read the text or study the lesson. Remind them during this independent work to look for details that confirm or challenge the answers from their interviews. By anchoring to prior knowledge, they have been primed to look closely and find details.

When to Use
- Before a new unit or lesson to activate prior knowledge
- Before conducting an experiment to make predictions
- As a check for understanding when relating new information to the previous day's lesson

Student-Made Anchor Charts

A helpful tool for using prior knowledge is an anchor chart created by students, for students. They can be charts and posters that stay in the classroom all year to display rules or assist with classroom management; or they can be tools the class uses during specific lessons, like a chart detailing the steps for writing a research essay. The idea is for students to have a voice in the creating process so they take ownership of the material. When students create the chart, they are clearly explaining, in their own words, what their prior knowledge is, giving you a great reference point for new material.

How to Use

Collectively
- A whole class can create anchor charts to display norms for collaboration and prompts for peer feedback.
- A group can create a metacognition anchor chart, generating terms to describe their various thought processes. Have students try to define the terms as they list them, and if you've talked to your students about DOK levels, have them try to identify which thought processes go with which level.
- A group can create a chart that develops over time, such as a list of vocabulary words. Students can write new words on colorful slips of paper to add continually to the chart.
- A group can create a chart listing the steps for solving word problems, or one categorizing the keywords for each mathematical operation (e.g. "in all," "sum," "difference," "take away," "product," "quotient," and so forth).

Individually
- A student can create an individual anchor chart on 8.5"x11" paper to keep as a reference sheet as part of his notes.
- Individually-created anchor charts can be more varied and detailed, and can be used as a formative assessment.

When to Use
- When you need to assess and activate prior knowledge to build on it
- To cater to multiple learning styles, since it is hands-on and visual, while still including words and numbers

Recommendations for Use:
Sometimes teachers create anchor charts on their own ahead of time, and then have students fill in the relevant information. This may work best for very complicated material, but we recommend that you allow students to construct the charts on their own whenever possible, so that the anchor chart can serve as a visual representation of the student's understanding. We also recommend allowing students to adapt their individual anchor charts to their own preferences, using pictures, words, or numbers as desired.

Challenge Questions:

1. Do you assess your students' prior knowledge?

2. Do your students get the chance to assess their own prior knowledge?

3. What are some pre-assessment activities you have found to be informative for both student and teacher?

4. Once you have an understanding of your students' prior knowledge, how do you anchor the new material to their understanding and experiences?

Discuss your responses with other teachers.

20. EMPOWER OWNERSHIP WITH MULTIPLICITY

Anchoring to activate prior knowledge goes hand-in-hand with providing multiplicity. To explore any idea more deeply, a student should be able to slow down, step back, and examine it from multiple perspectives. Prior knowledge is an important starting point, but to gain a more complete picture of any idea, it's necessary to step outside yourself and examine other perspectives.

During a 21-day expedition of the Bahamas blue holes, anthropologist Kenny Broad and diving expert Brian Kakuk teamed up to combine their expertise and maximize discovery. Together with archaeologist Michael Pateman, they recovered 800-year-old human remains, which helped them to understand the rituals of an indigenous people who had once used the blue hole as a burial ground. They teamed up with experts in other fields to get a more complete understanding of the underwater caves. They worked with ornithologist and paleontologist David Steadman, who identified the fossils of 35 previously unknown animal species that they had found in the depths of a blue hole. They worked with geo-chemist Peter Swart to extract and examine a cross section of an underwater stalagmite and found clues to the history of the earth's climate. Looking at blue holes through the lenses of multiple disciplines gave everyone a deeper understanding (PBS, 2013).

Provide Multiple Perspectives

Replicate this multidisciplinary experience for your students during DOK 3 and 4 lessons. Help them see that historians, psychologists, novelists, feminists, journalists—all of us—are looking at the same world, interpreting it in varying ways. Encourage students to make connections by providing multiple texts on a topic. If you're teaching math, bring in the financial pages and challenge students to find examples of fractions, percentages, exponents, and statistics. If you're teaching Shakespearean literature, provide supplemental historical texts from the Elizabethan Age, or find sociological research on family feuds that you can juxtapose with the Montague and Capulet families from *Romeo and Juliet*. Synthesizing information from multiple sources shows students how limitless their learning can be, leads to a cohesive, organized understanding that is truly the student's own, and it gives them practice in a skill they'll need for today's high-stakes tests.

Tip: If your regular curriculum is too time-crunched to include many of these types of cross-disciplinary lessons, you can still use this strategy to create enrichment activities for students who have finished their work ahead of time. This way you're leading them into more complex thinking on the topic being covered by everyone, rather than keeping them busy with more of the same type of work they have just finished.

Common Core Connection

Read the following Common Core State Standard. Presenting students with cross-disciplinary perspectives on a topic can help them to distance themselves and enter strategic thinking, which is necessary in order to evaluate credibility and accuracy.

CCSS.ELA-LITERACY.SL.9-10.2
Integrate multiple sources of information presented in diverse media or formats (e.g., visually, quantitatively, orally) evaluating the credibility and accuracy of each source (CCSSI, 2016).

Provide Multiple Choices

Tests today measure more than surface-level understanding. They measure a student's ability to carefully read and analyze multiple pieces of information at once, and to make inferences and appreciate subtleties so they can choose the "best" answer from multiple "correct" answers. Practicing these skills during class doesn't mean you're "teaching to the test." It means you're teaching them to read closely and evaluate subtle differences in meaning. Explore several similar statements and practice choosing "best" answers as a class, so that students know how to look for implications and subtle differences in meaning as they read. Create formative assessments that have multiple "correct" answers but one "best" answer, so they can practice these skills on their own when the stakes are low. It will better prepare them for standardized tests. More importantly, it will teach them to think strategically.

Challenge questions:

1. Do you supplement the learning material with related media that provides an interesting perspective?

2. What keeps you from employing multiplicity more often? Do time constraints keep you from adding new, related information to deepen student thought?

3. How might you rewrite questions to add multiple texts, perspectives, and "correct" answers to your current curriculum without increasing the instructional time required?

4. How can you add multiple texts, perspectives, and "correct" answers to supplement your current curriculum as enrichment materials for students who finish tasks early?

Discuss your responses with other teachers.

21: EXTENDING TO DOK 4

The Big Picture

Take another look at the diagram from our blue hole metaphor (module 5). We have labeled the passageways that extend horizontally from the anoxic water level as DOK 4. It is fitting that these tunnels are not all necessarily deeper than the discoveries that can be made in the strategic DOK 3 zone. Instead, they are simply longer and more complex, extending possibly for miles into vast networks of passages to explore.

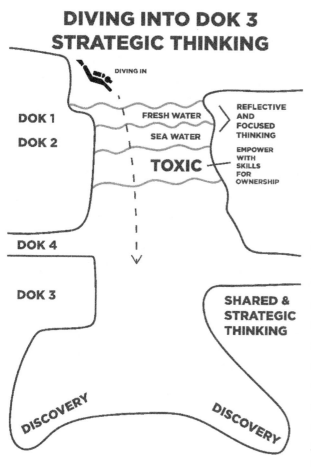

When working in DOK 3 and especially in DOK 4, we shift away from an effort to "cover" more material, which is often a necessary approach in the shallows of DOK 1 and 2, and embrace an effort to deepen understanding in one specific area. At DOK 3, that understanding becomes complex and personal. To extend it further, into DOK 4, the thinking must be sustained over a period of time. The student in DOK 4 must be given opportunities to explore the networks of connecting passageways and to transfer their learning to new situations. In a serendipitous twist, by abandoning the effort to move quickly and cover more material, students who reach DOK 4 end up extending their understanding to include vastly varied subjects and information. They cover much more material down in those connecting passageways than anyone on the surface could have guessed. In this way, DOK 4 allows students to see how a particular subject fits into the big picture, how it is connected and related to other ideas, and how it can be applied in real life.

Multiple Dives

We talked about taking a multi-step approach in module 9, but it's worth restating here because it applies particularly to DOK level 4. To engage in extended thinking, you must allot time to think on the subject multiple times, from different perspectives. Most of the material we've shared in modules 15-20 applies to time spent making a concerted thinking effort: studying, reading, note-taking, discussing. But it is especially important in DOK 4 to include periods of "incubation time" for the brain to re-organize new information before beginning the concerted thinking effort once more, through a new lens of understanding. Stretching a project out over multiple days or weeks—or even just revisiting a topic later in the same day or after a lunch break—helps the brain to absorb the learning. The reflective and focused thinking skills from Modules 15-16 and the collaborative process from module 17 can then be used once again, this time to extend understanding even further.

> DOK 4 allows students to see how subjects connect in the big picture.

DOK 4 Is For Everyone

Learners at every level can reach extended strategic thinking. *What Intelligence Tests Miss* by Keith E. Stanovich argues that people with high IQs are just as likely as anyone else to search for easy answers rather than thinking deeply. More important to real-world success than intelligence are certain mental dispositions that come from effort and experience, dispositions such as "the tendency to collect information before making up one's mind, the tendency to seek various points of view before coming to a conclusion, the disposition to think extensively about a problem before responding, the tendency to calibrate the degree of strength of one's opinions to the degree of evidence available, the tendency to think about the future consequences before taking action, the tendency to explicitly weight pluses and minuses of a situation before making a decision, and the tendency to seek nuance and avoid absolutism" (Stanovich, 2010). In other words, the ability to think deeply is more important to success than raw intelligence, and it can be practiced and learned and become a "tendency" or a "disposition." With practice, anyone can make deep thinking a habit.

DOK 4 Is For High-Ability Students

We just said DOK 4 is for everyone, and it is. But it is an especially useful tool for engaging high-ability students who might otherwise get bored. If you struggle to differentiate your instruction, make use of DOK 4 to keep everyone on the same page while allowing those who are ready to go deeper. For example, your freshmen biology students are studying inherited traits, and a few students have mastered the DOK 2 understanding before others. Rather than assigning them more Level 1 or 2 worksheets for extra credit, give the advanced students—and any student who is interested—a few related case studies to read and compare. Throughout the unit on genetic traits, allow them to work on this extra project whenever they happen to be ahead or have extra time. Give them the opportunity to turn in an essay or other project for extra credit, with a deadline that is at the end of the class's study of genetic traits. This means they will be working intermittently on the project over multiple days, and they will begin to understand their regular coursework on gene traits through the lens of the related case studies they are reading. This deepens their understanding of the subject while still keeping them engaged and on the same "pace" with the rest of the class.

Mix It Up with Cross-Content Projects

To facilitate DOK 4 thinking, it is helpful to provide cross-content projects or texts. Educators in Massachusetts developed a "financial literacy" unit in their English Language Arts curriculum (Massachusetts ESE, 2014). Financial literacy might be expected fodder for a math class, but to consider economics and finances verbally, through writing an essay about how money works or studying a text about the history of stock investing, adds an invaluable layer of understanding beyond the worlds of math and business. There are so many directions a student could go in a project like this: studying the causes of economic recession, reading up on the collapse of Enron, writing a personal reflection about their own financial priorities and goals. DOK 4 fosters unlimited creativity.

Here in DOK 4 the importance of autonomy becomes especially pronounced. The more choice a student has in choosing a direction for a cross-content project, the better. Remember, students at this level of thought need to be given models to aspire to, not blueprints to adhere to (module 10). In addition to looseness in the directions of the teacher, DOK 4 thinking also benefits from a relaxed timeline. Perhaps set a final deadline of a few weeks, but within that timeframe allow students to adjust the time they spend on different portions of a project. As long as they are able to show that they are making progress, they will benefit from the ability to create their own plan for accomplishing the work, choosing to spend additional time on research or more time on revising an essay.

Cross-Content Projects

Here are a few suggested cross-content projects that could encourage DOK 4 thinking:

1. **Multiple Viewpoints** - Read texts by multiple authors from the same time period or social context and challenge students to write an essay or poem, or create a video, comparing their attitudes, lifestyles, voices, or responses to a historic event.

2. **Word Families** - If you are studying a specific set of verbs in a language class, allow students to choose a verb and find words that are related to it in other languages or across disciplines. For example, the French verb *naitre*, "to be born" can be linked to all kinds of words, like "prenatal," "Renaissance," "native," "naive," "natural," and "nation." Challenge students to research the origins of a group of related words and trace how their meanings have changed over time across different cultures.

3. **Extended Collaboration** - Organize a group project so that each student is exploring a subject through a different lens. For example, in a project on World War II, one student could explore the role of women, one could explore the role of espionage, one could study Hitler's biography, and so on. All students in the group could come together to present an illustrated timeline or video that brings together key events and people from all three areas.

4. **Short Story Presentation** - Have students write a narrative short story that establishes plot, character, setting, sensory details, and dialogue. The writing should convey a theme through characters, actions, and images. Students should use varied word choices and sentence fluency to make writing interesting. Then have students present their narratives in small groups, demonstrating effective use of style, eye contact, tone, and adequate volume to maintain audience interest and attention.

5. **Ted Talk Response Video** - Assign students a Ted Talk video to watch, and challenge them to create their own video response that uses evidence to evaluate or rebut the Ted Talk.

Look back at the standards you identified as DOK 4 as you worked through module 8. Create extended strategic thinking activities that will correlate to these standards. Use the space below to brainstorm possible cross-content project ideas you could suggest to your students, which will correlate to those specific DOK 4 standards. But remember, for DOK 4 it's best to give students freedom to choose a topic within a specific subject area.

Challenge Questions:

1. Do you reserve DOK 4 thinking for high-ability students, or do all your students engage in this level of thinking?

2. Do you recognize and harness the power of DOK 4 for differentiating instruction?

3. Think of a few cross-content projects you could add to a unit you currently teach.

Discuss your responses with other teachers.

PART 3 TAKEAWAYS

- Students need to be overtly taught strategies and steps for effortful thinking work.
- Metacognition—thinking about thinking—allows students to "zoom out" and examine their own cognition so they can think strategically.
- Students need a common language for discussing thought processes, clear systems for focused thinking, and a common language for collaboration.
- Balance anchoring with multiplicity.
- Students need to assess their own prior knowledge so they can explore multiple topics and make connections.
- Students need practice evaluating multiple correct answers.
- Extending strategic thinking creates an opportunity for enrichment and engages students at all ability levels.

List additional takeaways below.

CONCLUSION

We hope this field guide has proved helpful for your professional growth. Looking through the "Depth of Knowledge spectacles," we believe you can guide your students into a daily practice of strategic thinking that will help them succeed throughout their lives. Cultivate a classroom environment that focuses on the thought process and allows strategic thinking to take place. Bring students through the effortful thinking work of reflecting and focusing by teaching metacognitive skills and systems. Give them the tools for effective thinking with collaborative norms that enable productive feedback. Anchor discussions in their prior knowledge, and make connections between multiple ideas to allow them to think critically, extending the strategic thinking to enrich the learning whenever possible.

During the writing of this book, we, the authors, were cognizant of the various levels of thought as we engaged in them. We learned a bit of basic information about how the brain works (level 1) and began to understand the structure and relationships between all four of Webb's Depth of Knowledge categories (level 2). We put forth a concerted effort, engaging in **reflective thinking** and **focused thinking**, taking notes and organizing our thoughts. But what really helped us to break into strategic (level 3) thinking was collaboration. The concerted effort we had each made toward reflecting and focusing made our **shared thinking** effective. It enabled us to make connections we had not before, to bounce ideas off one another, and it made thinking about Depth of Knowledge exciting for us. The length of time it took to write this book then pushed us into extended strategic thought (level 4). The ebb and flow of concerted effort balanced with times of rest while our minds wandered helped us to connect our ideas about Depth of Knowledge to the seemingly unrelated field of underwater diving. Our brains worked on this book while we went running and cooked dinner and slept. The insights we had while writing this book came from the connecting of big ideas and the extending of our thought into exciting new fields as we each went about our lives, seeing new ideas through the lens of the work we were doing. But these insights—the connecting and extending—would have been impossible without the repeated, methodical, effortful, skillful work of reflecting and focusing on whatever new information we had learned. We hope you too will find joy in the process of thinking strategically about your instruction.

Breaking through the toxic barrier to strategic thinking requires a harmonious balance of skilled work with times of cognitive exploration. We wish you the best of luck as you work to empower your students with the skills they need to take ownership of their thinking. Thank you for the work you do each day to create a new generation of engaged, insightful, lifelong learners.

REFERENCES

Abrahamson, E. and Freedman, D. H. (2006). *A perfect mess: The hidden benefits of disorder.* New York: Little, Brown and Company.

ACT. (2006). *Reading between the lines: What the act reveals about college readiness in reading.* Retrieved from http://achievethecore.org/content/upload/act_reading_between_the_lines_research_ela.pdf

Alliance of Community Trainers (2016). "Power". *Organizing for Power.* Retrieved in 2016 from http://organizingforpower.org/power-2/

Brooks, D. (2011). *The Social Animal.* New York: Random House.

Cash, R. M. (2011). *Advancing differentiation: thinking and learning for the 21st century.* Minneapolis, MN: Free Spirit Publishing.

CCSSI. (2016). All common core state standards retrieved from http://www.corestandards.org

Coleman, D. (2014). Delivering opportunity. The College Board. Video retrieved from https://www.youtube.com/watch?v=MSZbPJbXwMI

Covey, S. R. (1989). *The seven habits of highly effective people.* New York: Franklin Covey Co., Simon & Schuster.

DeBono Group, The. (2016). *Six thinking hats.* Retrieved in 2016 from http://www.debonogroup.com/six_thinking_hats.php?gclid=CjwKEAjwp-S6BRDj4Z7z2IWUhG8SJAAbqbF3NNuPJBdMrUx_ytpqdRo7ruFcMW8NeUIHm1YmRNhldhoCz6Dw_wcB

DOK Word Wheel: No original source found, as this image is shared freely in educational circles.

Druckerman, P. (2012). *Bringing up bébé: One american mother discovers the wisdom of french parenting.* New York: Penguin Press.

EL Education (2012). *Austin's butterfly: Building excellence in student work.* Retrieved from https://vimeo.com/38247060

EL Education (2012). *Grappling with Complex Informational Text.* Retrieved from https://vimeo.com/54007714

EngageNY (2016). A resource for finding complex text. Retrieved in 2016 from engageny.org

Finlay, S. and Leeson, A. (2014). *Integrating complex reading into classroom instruction* (PowerPoint slides). Retrieved from https://learningconnection.doe.in.gov/

Hess, K. K. (2009). *Hess' cognitive rigor matrix & curricular examples: applying webb's depth-of-knowledge levels to bloom's cognitive process dimensions – ELA.* Retrieved from http://static.pdesas.org/content/documents/M1-Slide_22_DOK_Hess_Cognitive_Rigor.pdf

Hess, K. K. (2012, February 2). *Cognitive rigor-webb's depth of knowledge, parts 1-3.* (Ledyard PS Video). Retrieved from https://www.youtube.com/watch?v=YiUh-hjqmRU

History Alive! (2007). *America: history of our nation—interactive reading and notetaking study guide, adapted version, 2nd ed.* Prentice Hall.

I Six Sigma (2016). *Determine the root cause: 5 whys.* Retrieved in 2016 from
    https://www.isixsigma.com/tools-templates/cause-effect/determine-root-cause-5-whys/

Kakuk, B. (2016) *Blue holes and underwater caves of the Bahamas.* Bahamas Caves Research Foundation.
    Retrieved in 2016 from http://www.bahamascaves.com/

Marzano, R. (2010). *The highly engaged classroom.* Bloomington, IN: Marzano Research Laboratory.

Massachusetts ESE. (2014). *The massachusetts curriculum development project.* Video retrieved in 2016
    from https://www.youtube.com/watch?v=rzpeLQMKLKc

Maxwell, J. C. (2003). *Thinking for a change: 11 ways highly successful people think.* New York: Warner
    Business Books.

NEWSELA (2016). Nonfiction literacy and current events. Retrieved in 2016 from newsela.com

New Tech Network (2016). *Agency scoring rubric.* Retrieved in 2016 from
    https://www.newtechnetwork.org/services/resources/ntn-student-learning-outcomes-and-
    rubrics

Ogle, R. (2007). *Smart world.* Boston: Harvard Business School Press.

Olsen, A. (1998). *Poems and prose from the old english.* London: Yale University Press.

Overseas Schools Advisory Council, U.S. Department of State. (2004). Norms of collaborative work.
    Count me in: Developing inclusive international schools, 4ᵗʰ ed. chapter 5. Retrieved from
    http://www.state.gov/m/a/os/43984.htm

PBS Nova. *(2013). Extreme cave diving.* Retrieved in 2016 from
    http://www.pbs.org/wgbh/nova/earth/extreme-cave-diving.html

Pink, Daniel H. (2009). *Drive.* New York: Penguin Group.

Rutherford, M. (2013). *The artisan teacher: A field guide to skillful teaching.* Weddington,
    NC: Rutherford Learning Group, Inc.

Schwartz, K. (April 19, 2016). How 'productive failure' in math class helps make lessons stick.
    MindShift. Retrieved from http://ww2.kqed.org/mindshift/2016/04/19/how-productive-
    failure-for-students-can-help-lessons-stick/

Stanovich, K. E. (2009). *What Intelligence Tests Miss: The Psychology of Rational Thought.* New Haven:
    Yale University Press.

Strauss, V. (June 1, 2016). Civil rights icon james meredith: 'we are in a dark age of american public
    education'. *The Washington Post.* Retrieved from
    https://www.washingtonpost.com/news/answer-sheet/wp/2016/06/01/civil-rights-icon-james-
    meredith-we-are-in-a-dark-age-of-american-public-
    education/?postshare=7861464816664428&tid=ss_fb

Tough, P. (2016). *Helping children succeed: What works and why.* Boston: Houghton Mifflin Harcourt.

Webb, N. (Presenter). (2013). *Dr. norman webb's dok overview.* WebbAlign. Video retrieved from
    http://www.webbalign.org/dok-training.html

Wiggins, G. (September 2012). Seven keys to effective feedback. *ASCD Educational Leadership*, 70, 10-
    16.

William, D. (2011). *Embedded formative assessment.* Bloomington, IN: Solution Tree Press.

Wong, H. K. and Wong, R. T. (2009). The first days of school: How to become an effective teacher.
    Mountain View, CA: Harry K. Wong Publications, Inc.

Made in the USA
Coppell, TX
01 September 2021